Prokofiev

Prokofiev

Thomas Schipperges

translated by J M Q Davies
introduced by Nicholas Kenyon

HAUS PUBLISHING · LONDON

First published in German in the Rowohlts monographien series
© 1995, 2001 Rowohlt Taschenbuch Verlag GmbH

This English translation first published in Great Britain in 2003 by
Haus Publishing Limited
32 Store Street
London WC1E 7BS

English translation © J M Q Davies, 2003
Introduction © Nicholas Kenyon, 2003
Epilogue © Peter Sheppard Skærved, 2003

The moral right of the authors has been asserted

A CIP catalogue record for this book
is available from the British Library

ISBN 1-904341-32-2 (paperback)
ISBN 1-904341-34-9 (hardback)

Designed and typeset in Albertina at Libanus Press, Marlborough

Printed and bound by Graphicom in Vicenza, Italy

Front cover: painting of Sergey Prokofiev, 1945
courtesy of the Lebrecht Music Collection
Back cover: drawing courtesy of the Lebrecht Music Collection

Contents

Introduction

Will the real Sergey Prokofiev please stand up? Who is he? There is the wild innovator of the *Second Symphony*, the brazen noise-merchant of the *Scythian Suite*, the cool classicist of the *Classical Symphony*, the gentle educationalist of *Peter and the Wolf*, the stern socialist-realist of the *Ode to the End of the War*, the cheerful satirist of *The Love of Three Oranges*, the historical pageant-maker of *Ivan the Terrible* . . . the list, as this fascinating biography makes clear, could be endless.

Surely never, even in the turbulent history of music in the twentieth century, has a composer turned so many different faces to the world as did Prokofiev. This was not duplicity, nor was it the same kind of stylistic chameleon-like behaviour as that of his great contemporary Stravinsky. Indeed the contrast between these two great composers is that Stravinsky, whatever musical idiom he chose to work in, always sounds distinctively Stravinskian, an enormous individuality submerging the stylistic framework, while Prokofiev so often successfully seems to hide his own musical character behind the mask of cleverly assumed style.

The mask: that could serve as a metaphor for the whole of Prokofiev's difficult, often brilliant but ultimately tragic career. Did he ever know who he really was? Or did he take on, with supreme skill and technical command, a whole range of musical languages and discourse so cleverly in them that people could easily miss the real composer beneath? This is where politics becomes central to this story, for the mask was a vital and necessary piece of armour for any composer who had to struggle against – and in the end, in the Prokofiev's case, fall victim to – the repressive persecution of a regime that claimed to know what music should be. Another great contemporary of his, Shostakovich, wore the mask outwardly, but behind it managed to say things of extraordinary pertinence and critical relevance to the regime in which he worked. You could sense when he was trying to sound hollow, and when he explored real depths. With Prokofiev, that is not always so easy.

Of course, in the 20th century it has become increasingly difficult for composers to follow a single stylistic line, and to believe that they are part of a great tradition. The melting-pot of the pre-First World War years in which Prokofiev's musical upbringing took place was one of the most cathartic in musical history, and it gave rise to so many different idioms and languages as the years progressed that any composer as clever and as resourceful as Prokofiev would have wanted to explore them and to impress with his command of them. He wanted to shock too, that is clear: his early autobiography speaks approvingly of the scandal caused by his *Second Piano Concerto* and the savage impact made by the *Scythian Suite*.

When Prokofiev left his homeland and worked in America and Europe, he was exposed to the full range of vital musical languages that were being developed. In Paris he felt the need to be exciting and dissonant, but later turned to the 'new simplicity' of pieces such as the *Second Violin Concerto* which was premièred in Spain, and which had strong echoes of his Russian folk roots. But just as Prokofiev never really felt at home abroad, and in the end decided to return to Russia, so too you feel he never became completely at home with the musical idioms he espoused. With one possible exception: the piano music that he wrote for himself to play, whether simply elegant or dazzlingly complex, has a stylistic poise which is perhaps born of his own ownership of it in performance.

It is also difficult to be sure why Prokofiev returned to Russia: the simple claim he made that he wanted to hear the Russian language again seems inadequate, and it has been suggested that he was calculating enough to think that, while as pianist abroad he would be in the shadow of Rakhmaninov and as a composer abroad in the shadow of Stravinsky, once he returned to Russia in 1936 just after Shostakovich had been condemned, he would have no rivals.

If that was the calculation it was a short-sighted one, for Prokofiev himself eventually fell victim in 1948 to exactly the same sort of denunciation as Shostakovich, even though he had devoted himself to writing such Soviet works as *Hail to Stalin* and the *Ode to the End of the War* (though the latter was oddly included by the authorities on a first list of proscribed works). A final attempt to reinvent himself in a still more straightforward style in his opera *The Story of a Real Man* was judged to be fruitless, and Prokofiev lived disappointed and inactive till he died, by a strange irony on the same day as Stalin, 5 March 1953.

Yet his career was by no means a failure. Prokofiev has established himself as one of the most enduring and characteristic of twentieth-century composers, and in the end it is his very variety that makes him typical of his age. Several of his works are among the most popular pieces of classical music written in the last hundred years: think of the countless performances of *Peter and the Wolf*, or the way that *Romeo and Juliet* has become more than a ballet – it has become the stuff of advertising soundtracks and sports theme tunes, a sure measure of immortality in this fragile age. Many more works appear regularly in concert programmes across the world: at the BBC Proms, among the great symphonies that conductors want to perform, *Prokofiev's Fifth* ranks very high. The 50th anniversary of his death, celebrated in 2003, will doubtless cause many rarer works to be revived as well. And if subsequent imitation is one measure of a great composer's success, then Prokofiev is up there with the greatest: just listen to the finale of the *Classical*

Symphony and then to the fugue from Benjamin Britten's *Young Person's Guide to the Orchestra* . . .

This biography explores the dilemmas and puzzles that lie at the heart of Prokofiev's life and music: it is thus about much more than one composer. It is about the problems of composing music in a multilingual, multi-cultural age in which mass communication has more than ever made every development available to all. It raises vitally important questions about music and politics, music and personality, music and identity.

NICHOLAS KENYON
Director of the BBC Proms since 1996
Controller, BBC Proms, Live Events, and TV Classical Music
His books include Simon Rattle: From Birmingham to Berlin (*Faber*)
and Musical Lives, *a compilation of entries from the* Dictionary of
National Biography (*OUP*)

Problematic Prokofiev

Notoriously, historical figures have many faces. The perspective changes with one's point of view, and received traditions distort the picture and bring marginal shadows or contradictions into focus like a lens. Anyone getting involved in the study of Prokofiev today is confronted by a host of transmitted preconceptions and conventions. For the picture of the composer, of his personality and work, is not only incomplete, it is, one might say, doubly fractured. On the one hand there are the distinctive, and much debated, attitudes of East and West towards Prokofiev's work in relation to his biography. Soviet musical history tended to ignore, if not actively to denigrate, Prokofiev the musician active in Western modernist circles. Conversely, literature about him in the West long had difficulty with the more simple, and ostensibly politically determined, idiom of Prokofiev the Soviet composer. Today these divergent attitudes appear to have been broadly resolved. As early as the 1950s Gerald Abraham sought to prove the essential unity of Prokofiev's work, suggesting that '"simplicity" had always been a significant feature of his style,'[1] a perspective which went against the prevailing current at the time. Since then there has been broad acceptance of the position which sees a 'measure of continuity' throughout his work.[2]

Beyond this official and oppositional picture of Prokofiev, in both the East and West there was and is a consensus as to the value of only a small portion of his work among the informed musical public. This is the second dichotomy in the reception history of Prokofiev. Works like the opera *The Story of a Real Man* or the ballet *The Stone*

HISTORICAL PERSPECTIVE

Sergey Prokofiev by Pyotr Konchalovsky, 1934

Flower, are among Prokofiev's few pieces of genuine 'official' music, in which he attempted to subordinate his own aesthetic impulses to political expediency.

Significant early compositions such as the cantata *Seven, They are Seven*, as well as masterpieces like the *Second Symphony*, and the opera *The Fiery Angel* or those 'unwieldy' late works, the *Sixth Symphony* and the *Sinfonia Concertante for Cello and Orchestra*, encountered as much hostility in the Soviet Union as protracted indifference in the West.

Coincidentally it is precisely those of Prokofiev's works which in the East were highly regarded as models of socialist realism that have also enjoyed uninterrupted favour with Western audiences: the musical fairy-tale *Peter and the Wolf*, the ballet music *Romeo and Juliet* and *Cinderella*, the *Alexander Nevsky* cantata, the *Second Violin Concerto* and the *Fifth Symphony*.

As early as 1933, on one of his return visits to the Soviet Union, Prokofiev remarked that: *I don't want to be esteemed by Soviet listeners just for the march from the 'Three Oranges' and the gavotte from the 'Classical Symphony'.*[3] And in the United States in the 1940s the composer's popularity rested above all on the success of that 'charming little musical fairy-tale *Peter and the Wolf* . . . In American record catalogues . . . Prokofiev ranked above Mozart and not far below Beethoven and Tchaikovsky.'[4] In the East people are as little troubled by the fact that *The Love for Three Oranges* is the major work of the composer's years in America, as they are in the West by the fact that *Peter and the Wolf* constitutes not only an educational manual about orchestral instruments, but also a paradigm of correct composition on the principles of socialist realism. In this instance the ideologically determined double image of Prokofiev turns out to be an illusion. But as regards the tendency to adopt an eclectic mode in assessing his music, little has changed even today.

Clearly a complete picture of Prokofiev from a single perspective is not to be attained. His personality is evidently too complex and the tensions that typify his work too fundamental. Prokofiev, after all, lived through an astounding period in Russia's history, from the reign of Tsar Nicholas II through Lenin to the death of Stalin, he witnessed an epoch torn asunder by two revolutions and two world wars.

The son of an estate manager, Sergey Sergeyevich Prokofiev spent his childhood in a Ukraine moulded by Tsarist social structures. As a student in St Petersburg he found himself in the midst of the revolutionary ferment of the years following 1905. His education

Socialist realism is effectively a formula; it is difficult to define, but encapsulates elements which, it was announced, artists needed to balance in order that their art fulfil its social and revolutionary obligations. Art should provide positive role models looking forward to an optimistic socialist future, in the most 'realist' manner possible. This dogma was first announced by Gorky, Bukharin, and Zdhanov at the 1934 Soviet Writers Conference. One might argue that, in concert with its antithesis, the much maligned 'Formalism', socialist realism encouraged a suspicion and paranoia in the artistic community exactly matched in the contemporaneous rise of McCarthyism.

Any form of pessimism was completely outside its remit, so works such as Prokofiev's less than optimistic *Sixth Symphony* and the sexual violence of Shostakovich's *Lady Macbeth of the Mtsensk District* were summarily condemned as anti-social. Melodies had to be hummable, keys had to be major. This dogma was exactly that imposed on the European émigré composers working in Hollywood in the 1930s. The MGM producer Irving Thalberg actually issued a memo to his resident composers that read: 'From the above date forward, no music in an MGM film is to contain a minor chord.' Andre Previn reported that it was still bolted to the wall of the music department twenty-five years later.

SOCIALIST REALISM

Tsar Nicholas II   Vladimir Ilych Lenin

at the Conservatory was marked by disagreements with the teachers and rejection of the mental attitudes of the older generation. *I sent all that nonsense to the devil with my 'Scythian Suite'.*[5] Prokofiev also became involved in the great explosion of Futurism in the arts in Russia. He was receptive to all the new artistic trends and '-isms' of his time, without ever allowing himself to be completely captured by them. He set the mystically charged poems of the Symbolists to music as readily as the transparent lyrics of the Acmeists. He disagreed with Skryabin early on, quickly distancing himself from him. And as he later proudly emphasized, he was the first to perform Schoenberg publicly in Russia.[6] He associated with the pre-revolutionary avant-garde movements in Russia, bent on shocking the bourgeoisie.[7] The Futurist poet Vladimir Mayakovsky 'dedicated his poem *War and the World* to him, inscribing it 'To the President of the musical half of the globe from the President of the poetic half of the globe, to Prokofiev from Mayakovsky.'[8] Prokofiev spent the summer of 1917, the months between the February and the October Revolutions, in retreat at a health resort in the country. There he

Futurism. On 20 February 1909, Filippo Marinetti published his 'Futurist Manifesto' in *Le Figaro*, Paris. The growl of the automobile, he wrote, surpassed Michelangelo in its beauty. In Russia, Futurism's liveliest progeny was 'Cubo-Futurism', the poetic and artistic movement founded by the radical artists and writers who had been in Paris before the revolution. Mayakovsky spent time with Marinetti when he visited Russia in 1914, and was profoundly influenced by him. One might say that, after the Revolution, this Russian Futurist movement was subsumed into the 'constructivist' movement. The most famous early Italian Futurist composer, Luigi Russolo gave concerts in Milan (1914) and Paris (1921), in which his *intonamuri* or noise-makers, inflamed the audience to riot – they stormed the stage and attacked the performers. His musical 'Manifesto' was published four years after Marinetti's; it suggested the division of the octave into fifty microtones and classified various non-musical sounds. Russolo's ideas probably had the biggest influence on the Parisian composers in the 1920s and, by extension, on some of the work of the Russian experimental composers of the period, such as Mossolov and the young Prokofiev. Perhaps Futurism's greatest impact on the performing arts was in its blurring of the divisions between the various disciplines, and its manipulation of the media's presentation of its provocative events, very much anticipating the modern inter-relationship between art and publicity.

composed his *Classical Symphony*. Should this be taken as evidence of political alienation, youthful naivety, indifference rising from intellectual arrogance, or calculated independent-mindedness? Or was it perhaps 'an expression of visionary optimism about the future . . . , that is, already in 1917 a document attesting to the humanist Prokofiev'?[9]

Making a realistic assessment of the prospects for an artist during revolutionary times, Prokofiev went abroad during the Bolshevik revolution. Travelling on a Soviet passport, he went for a limited period, not as an emigrant. His concern to maintain contact with his homeland and keep open the possibility of returning never wavered. For two decades Prokofiev was a wanderer between different worlds. He composed operas and full-scale symphonies, genres which in the European West by then seemed

Vladimir Mayakovsky (1893–1930), a founder of the Russian Futurist movement, became the most prominent and influential Soviet poet and theorist. He was also an artist, designing revolutionary posters, and an actor. His fame was international. From their first encounter in 1918, Prokofiev and Mayakovsky were close friends, bound by a mutual admiration for one another's talent and the conventions of Futurism. Mayakovsky glorified the revolution and its leaders but he also castigated the new Soviet bureaucracy for its old petit-bourgeois conformism, in satires and utopian comedies.

Stalin's rise to power in the late 1920s saw an end to artistic freedoms and initiated a repressive and turbulent political-cultural period that affected all Soviet artists. Mayakovsky came under intense ideological pressure and found it increasingly difficult to reconcile his artistic independence with the conformist demands of the growing cultural bureaucracy. He was persecuted by the RAPP (Russian Association of Proletarian Writers) who stigmatized him as a 'class enemy'. On 14 April 1930 he committed suicide.

to have lost their currency. His music was very much at the centre of the operatic reforms introduced by director Vsevolod Meyerhold, who was attempting to find a contemporary Soviet idiom for the stage beyond conventional realism, rhetorical patriotism and escapist exoticism. In 1927 Prokofiev once again returned to his homeland where he was received enthusiastically. Memories of the warmth of this reception remained with him and in 1933 he expressed his intention to return to Russia permanently. In 1936 he gave up his apartment in Paris and from then on resided in the Soviet Union. In 1938 Prokofiev was allowed to travel abroad one last time.

Prokofiev's was a slow homecoming, yet his return occurred in the context of widespread artistic pluralism in the Soviet Union of the 1920s and innumerable cultural exchanges between East and West. It was the final phase of a complex process protracted over many years, and came at a time immediately before the height of the Stalinist terror and the first intensive campaigns against all the arts including music, which eventually led to purges across the entire field of cultural endeavour. As an integral part of Soviet musical life, indeed for a long time as its dominant musical personality, Prokofiev found himself celebrated and persecuted in equal measure. He did not misunderstand what initially only took the form of veiled threats, and actively engaged in seeking the folk music of his country together with other Russian traditions. Compositions expressing sympathy for the revolution and the socialist state ensued, still without substantial concessions to mass taste, but in the face of vicious personal attacks in 1948, he finally submitted to formal and stylistic restrictions.

Prokofiev's hands at the piano keyboard

Prokofiev was not a dissident, in either the artistic or the political sense, and unlike Shostakovich, he never became an icon of the 'unbroken greatness' of Soviet music. 'His conduct in various situations,' according to Alfred Schnittke, 'suggests that he was a cool, meticulously precise person who assessed everything and protected himself from the blinding theatre of life by means of a sort of "intelligent irony". . . This non-acceptance of a "surreally" frightening reality, this refusal to bow, this unwillingness to resort to tears, this determination not to yield to abuse, all this seemed to offer him salvation. Sadly this salvation was an illusion, as the more important invisible and essential part of this athletic, business-like Prokofiev repressed what he found insuperable so deeply, to the extent that it drove him to an early death at the age of sixty-one.'[10]

Detachment became a form of protection, and it was not only from the political pressures in the Soviet Union that Prokofiev sought to withdraw in this way. The objectifying of relationships, which was interpreted by many as arrogance, was a significant part of his approach to life. With this knowledge the occasionally intense attachment of the otherwise religiously indifferent composer to the teachings of Christian Science becomes more understandable. In her instructional work *Science and Health*, Mary Baker Eddy, the

PERSECUTION

founder of this religious community, had expounded the unreality and powerlessness of all material being when set against the only true reality, that of the human spirit united with God.[11] The composer was fascinated by this pragmatic faith in spiritual recognition of the potential for transcendental health. The notion that this alone might empower individual consciousness to transcend the burden of external vicissitudes must have appealed a good deal to Prokofiev's self-assertive instincts: *Depression is a lie of the mortal mind, consequently it cannot have power over me, for I am the expression of Life, ie; divine activity.*[12] Going on from here, Prokofiev jotted down (in English) his theory of creative action in twenty propositions:

1 *I am the expression of Life, i.e. of divine activity.*

2 *I am the expression of spirit which gives me power to resist what is unlike spirit.*

3 *My fidelity grants me uninterrupted adherence to all what* [sic] *is true.*

4 *I am the expression of love which sustains my constant interest in my work.*

5 *My individuality is given me to express beauty.*

6 *As I am the expression of Mind, I am capable of vigorous creative thinking.*

7 *As I am the effect of the one great Cause, I ignore everything that does not proceed from this Cause.*

8 *I am the expression of joy, which is stronger than aught* [sic] *unlike it.*

9 *I am the expression of perfection, and this leads me to the perfect use of my time.*

10 *I am in possession of health, therefore I work with ease.*

11 *I have wisdom in order to constantly express it.*

12 *I am the image of Mind; this keeps me busy to express inspired thoughts.*

13 *I am honest to myself, and therefore will do the work which is the best.*

14 *As activity is my inherent quality, the desire to work is natural.*

15 *Whereas I am the expression of soul, I feel the necessity to express beauty.*

16 *I am spiritual, consequently vigorous.*

17 *Infinite Life is the source of my vitality.*

18 *At every moment I am alert to express beautiful thoughts.*

19 *I am eager to work, because action is the expression of Life.*

20 *I rejoice in spite of tribulations [which provide] the opportunity to prove the realities of life.*[13]

Schnittke has described such 'refusal to admit tragedy as the ultimate determinant of life' as, objectively, the tragedy of the composer's fate.[14]

Any attempt to provide a key to the broad stylistic palette of Prokofiev's oeuvre through biography can only be partially and superficially successful. It is the aim of his work to resist all rigid definitions, and to remain responsive to many layers of significance and open-ended in its conclusions.

Prokofiev himself described his compositions as 'polystylistic'. And we are not dealing here with periodically changing phases (conventionally Prokofiev's work, like that of all other composers, is divided into three periods), but rather with major tendencies discernible in his work which transcend all constraints of time and space and all traditional formal and generic boundaries: *First there is the classicizing tendency, originating in early childhood when I used to listen to my mother playing Beethoven's sonatas . . . The second tendency is toward innovation . . . At first this was a quest for a distinctive harmony, then it turned into a quest for a language to express strong emotions . . . Although with this tendency it is mainly a question of harmony, innovation in the melodic objectives, in the instrumentation and in the formal structure is also entailed. The third is the toccata, or if one prefers, the motoric tendency . . . The fourth is the lyric tendency . . . I would like to confine myself to these four tendencies, and to regard a fifth, the 'grotesque' . . . more as an extension of the aforementioned tendencies . . . When applied to my music, I would that the word 'grotesque' was replaced by the term 'jocose', or if one prefers, by three words suggesting its different levels of intensity: jest, laughter, mockery.*[15]

The panoramic spectrum of Prokofiev's work obstinately resists attempts at classification. Logic and lyricism, sharpness and jest, wit and contradiction are terms that capture tensions within an art suspended between avant-garde and adaptability, between obduracy and conciliation, between irony and profundity of meaning. Pluralism here becomes a sign of unity. *A composer must always seek new modes of expression . . . Each one of his works must have its own technique. If this is not the case, he will inevitably repeat himself, and that is always the beginning of the end.*[16]

Simplicity and complexity are both among the qualities that tend to be noticed in his music, no less frequently as criticism than as acknowledged strengths. Even before his real career as a composer had begun, when he was working on his Pushkin opera *The Feast in Time of Plague*, his friend Nikolay Myaskovsky advised him to 'give up the absurd and unnecessary attempt to write simply; better to write in your usual complicated way, but well.'[17]

Prokofiev himself felt it important to emphasize the simplicity of his art from the very beginning: *In everything I write I stick to two main principles, clarity in the presentation of my ideas, and laconic brevity, avoiding all that is superfluous in the expression.*[18] Of course Prokofiev composed some bizarre modulations, aggressive dissonances, and polytonal formations, and some sharp-edged themes and athematic melodic impulses, sometimes (perhaps most radically in the *Second Symphony*) bordering on atonality. But he never questioned the tonal foundation of his work. His conviction that the tonal system was the basis of music consequently exposed him to the opprobrium of many representatives of the new music.

Recognition of the outstanding technical ability that had allowed him to develop his very varied polymorphous art had also to contend with a degree of scepticism regarding this same stylistic pluralism. His technical skill and artistic curiosity were construed as indications of frivolity. And down to our day such moralizing has frequently characterized polemics over his music, even though it manifestly transcends reductions of what is new to simple dichotomies between Schoenberg and Stravinsky. *'Modern', that is a good word, but in your letter it occurs about fifteen times, and by the end it hovers over one's head like the threatening crack of a whip. One ought not to turn oneself into a thick journal, which gives a thought to the modern only because otherwise it would lose its subscribers.*[19]

Prokofiev liked orderliness and unambiguous objective structures, yet at the same time always avoided, 'closed systems'. He found the free atonal expressionism of Schoenberg's early piano pieces fascinating, but he regarded the twelve-tone technique itself as a theoretically academic construct. He let himself be caught up in the aesthetic revolt of the Futurists, but the Futurist manifestos, which are so personally revealing, *left me cold.*[20] In the Soviet context, Prokofiev believed he could go along with the notion of adjusting art to public taste, until the rigorous proscriptiveness of socialist realism forced him to conform. *I suspect that as soon as an artist attempts to formulate his own artistic logic to himself, he unwittingly restricts himself.*[21]

Throughout his entire life Prokofiev was governed by the urge to reach an audience with his work. Even his defiant gestures as the *enfant terrible* of Russian music, out to shock bourgeois sensibilities in the decade before the Revolution, should be understood as an attitude struck, or role played, for the benefit of the public. Prokofiev was a gambler; he gambled with the public too. From this point of view his music should be connected with the 'middle-brow music' which developed during the 1920s as an experimental alternative to the austere stylistic ideals of the new music. This 'middle-brow music' entailed rejection of traditional genres in favour of new possibilities in form and casting; it relinquished claims to the autonomy of art as a prerequisite for compositional freedom; it was fast-paced, not too highly idiosyncratic, and responsive to the needs of a utilitarian art designed for everyday enjoyment.[22] Yet it was precisely *great music* that was important to Prokofiev, great both *conceptually* and as regards *technical construction.*[23] From the outset his compositions took shape principally within the traditional genres of theatrical or autonomous concert music, opera, symphony, concerto, or sonata. In the Paris of the early 1920s it was his *Second Symphony* that provided a counterweight to the predominance of 'middle-brow music.'

On the other hand the *Overture on Hebrew Themes* is frankly an occasional piece. Prokofiev described it as *a work of little importance, quite as easy for the players as the audience.*[24] Initially he did not even want to acknowledge his overture by giving it an opus number. But even in a piece like this, he was at pains to adhere strictly to its musical tenets once he had established them. In response to a query he said *it had never occurred to me that in my 'Overture' Op 34 one might substitute a string instrument for the clarinet. Nor do I think this would be a happy innovation.*[25] He drew attention to the performance instructions and hints for interpretation which he had set *down in the score . . . with all possible precision.*[26]

'As Prokofiev's oeuvre approached completion, one was (and is) able to attend more to the various possible ways of reading one and the same work, tackled afresh a hundred times . . . , or to the innumerable anticipations of ideas in later works.'[27]

There is a correlation between the perfection and painstaking precision of Prokofiev's piano playing, and the strict economy and calculated effect which are the fundamental principles of his composing; in this of course, his was very similar to Bartok's playing and composing. Prokofiev's mania for altering, very like that of his teacher Rimsky-Korsakov, is a sign of his habitual scepticism and penchant for self-criticism. On occasion he would listen to individual chords from his own music with extreme attention. It is astounding how obstinately Prokofiev would pursue large-scale projects over years or decades, even when there were no concrete prospects of their ever being performed. A mode of expression aiming at comprehensibility, even the possibility of music as entertainment, were far from being incompatible with the notion that music should have its own aesthetic autonomy.

Prokofiev's activities also reflect the tensions between internationalism and national tradition. When abroad he always emphasized his firm devotion to his homeland, yet his relation to Russian national tradition is a thoroughly ambiguous one. In contrast to Stravinsky, Prokofiev almost never displayed the links with folklore in his music as a form of national exoticism, although the *Second Quartet* came close to this. Consequently, in his case it is not always easy to draw the line between natural folk influence and deliberate flavouring.[28] By the time Prokofiev embarked on his public musical career at the age of seventeen, music in Russia had, for the most part left any genuine connection with the 'folk spirit' well behind. Not only the academic tradition of Taneyev and Glazunov, but also Skryabin's universal mysticism, Rakhmaninov's drawing-room romanticism, and the technical brilliance of the young Stravinsky's sounds tended to show how strong the Russian links to European music had become. Prokofiev engaged with Haydn and Beethoven, or with Schumann and Chopin, or with Wagner and Reger. Only in his ballets *Ala and Lolli* and *The Buffoon* did he turn at this time, with Sergey Diaghilev's encouragement, to nationalist subject matter. In America and Paris, Russian themes ceased to play any part in his work for a considerable time. It was only his later increasing involvement with Soviet musical life that provided him with the incentive to reflect on Russian national tradition, almost as a conciliatory gesture. The political motivation is unmistakable of course. But if in his *Second String Quartet*, written at the time of the 'Great War for the Fatherland', or in some of his pieces for film and the stage, the composer made use of folk melodies, he did not do this solely in a spirit of patriotism. The folksong material could at the same time also be used to legitimate breaches of the strictly functional tonal system officially prescribed by the state.

Prokofiev strenuously maintained his individuality and intellectual independence: *I don't mind saying that in all essentials I am a student of my own ideas.*[29] He exposed himself continually to the stimuli and influences of his immediate environment, and succeeded in quickly assimilating new artistic currents, remaining independent, unprejudiced, and undogmatic. He was inherently an open-minded artist. But he was a conformist.

The stylistic changes in Prokofiev's work scarcely ever march in

SECOND QUARTET

step with historical currents. Even if his mode of composing never developed into a school, at least outside his own country, it often anticipated future developments. On occasion the very tradition-bound pragmatism of his music turned out to be tradition breaking. In place of Glazunov's academic suaveness he offered a bold strength and harmonic roughness, while in response to Rakhmaninov's sentimental routines he came up with the stylized simplicity and underlying light-heartedness of his *Classical Symphony*. He responded to the Promethean exaltations of Skryabinism with diatonic clarity and tightly knit forms, and to 'boneless'[30] Impressionism with regulated metrical periodicity and precisely organized sequential movements. In the context of Diaghilev's and Stravinsky's innovative ideas for the stage and the aesthetics of transience of 'Les Six',[31] he pursued his own ideas for opera and the full-scale symphony. And in the case of the mass culture of socialist realism he sought to appropriate its forms while using his own methods.

Prokofiev's diatonic linearity is a manifestation of a swing away from late Romantic modernism, a full decade before the comparable paradigm shift occurred in Western European music. His bi-tonal constructions are equally a means of defamiliarization, of escaping the dominant mode of alternating chords and melody. Prokofiev did not seek a return to the classical-romantic musical idiom, and his simplicity is a decidedly a 'new simplicity'.[32] Within it the experiences of contemporary music are both reflected and assessed. His intention with

Alexander Skryabin

these consciously adopted limitations is specifically to register his scepticism regarding the Romantic principle of emotional expressionism. *One should not forget that emotions understood by the present generation could seem strange and even ridiculous to the next generation of listeners.*[33]

The detached and self-conscious stance Prokofiev typically adopts in his music may be understood in terms of the concept of irony, irony as a refusal to be taken in and a defence against polarities, as revulsion at romantic excess and fear of metaphysical 'profundity'. Well versed in traditional technique, Prokofiev used various styles and registers in his art but contrived to make them serve his own ends. In this sense the flexibility and rhetorical adroitness of his idiom proved musically serviceable even in his contributions to Soviet utilitarian music. It is here, in the synthesis of 'seriousness' and 'jest' and the union of art and play, in the mask of stylization and the laconic idiom of 'as if', that the unmistakable qualities of Prokofiev's personality and art, so 'full of that strange raw-boned optimism',[34] transcending all tensions and contradictions, are to be located: between tradition and modernity, between audience-directedness and musical autonomy, between national consciousness and cosmopolitanism.

The opera *The Love for Three Oranges* is a work by a Russian composer, commissioned by an American theatre, based on material from an Italian poet, written in French. It was appropriate that at the International Music Festival in Duisburg in 1991, after the fall of the Berlin Wall, Prokofiev should be invoked in a call for a 'dialogue between European cultures',[35] in the presence of Lev Kopelev, an expatriate Russian poet, as well as numerous Soviet cultural functionaries.

But even as a symbol of unity the composer's personality and work are complex. Sergey Prokofiev always found himself falling between two stools. That is where, to quote Tucholsky, all significant people fall.

From a Composer's Youth

Prokofiev's autobiographical notes are a central document for the history of the composer's childhood and youth. His early personal and musical development could not be more cogently presented than in *Prokofiev on Prokofiev*.[36] The fact that it is based on original documentation – diaries, letters, reminiscences, notes, and newspaper reports – makes his account, in the words of the editor of the autobiography, Miralda Koslova, 'an unusually reliable document'.[37] Its authenticity has been stressed repeatedly. It may also be regarded as a personal submission by the composer: *Is it worth writing one's own autobiography – especially in such great detail? Of course it isn't worth it. The only disturbing thing is that if I don't write it, others will do so; and they will undoubtedly misrepresent a number of things.*[38] Putting aside his doubts, Prokofiev emphasized the documentary immediacy of his text, drawing attention to the source of his materials and his early plans to assemble them: *The urge to record various things in writing has been a distinctive trait in my character from early childhood . . . At twenty-one . . . I came to the decision that at an appointed time I would write my autobiography.*[39]

   In fact, the actual writing of Prokofiev's autobiography dates from very much later, between 1937 and 1939 (part one: *Childhood*) and between 1945 and 1949 (part two: *The Conservatory*). It underwent a complex process of revision, first with the publication of an abbreviated version in the journal *Soviet Music* (1941 and 1946),[40] then with the contributions of Mira Mendelson (based on the composer's dictation and material from the Prokofiev Archive), leading to a definitive text for the final edition of 1973. In the midst of war and sickness, divorce and Zhdanov's purges, the composer's personal and political fate coloured these notes in complicated ways. The retrospective point of view, looking back from the 1930s and 1940s, is thus part of their message. It is not so much the omission of events and facts pointed out in detail by the editor herself that is at issue. These can be corrected readily enough by recourse to other documents. What is of more interest is Prokofiev's reconstruction of his own personal and artistic development. It can scarcely be verified, and yet in the East and in the West alike it has influenced our image of the composer. Given Prokofiev's personal predicament, a newly arrived returnee to a Soviet Union in turmoil, it is understandable that in hindsight he had a tendency to stylize the past in his writing. This reminds us that, for all our admiration for the liveliness and frankness of Prokofiev the writer, we should on occasion regard these biographical notes with scepticism.

Prokofiev's autobiography begins with his father: *My father, Sergey Alexeyevich Prokofiev, was born in Moscow on 8 July 1948. This date refers to the old calendar. To convert it to the new calendar, this century twelve days must be added, which would make 20 July his birthday. But this date does not mean anything at all to me. The date fixed in my memory as a child was 8 July. On that day guests would come and visit us and the first watermelon would be ripe. If it had ripened earlier, we would save it for the great day. But if it ripened later, we used to say the melon had cheated us.*[41] His father's station in life, that of estate manager and family patriarch, emerges clearly, but his personality remains obscure. Sergey Alexeyevich Prokofiev was descended from a family of Moscow merchants, *wealthy people, although fairly uneducated.*[42] He attended the commercial school in Moscow and subsequently went on to take a course at the Agricultural Academy in Petrovik. As the manager of an estate, Sontsovka, in the Donezk district of the Ukraine, he was receptive to the latest industrial and agricultural innovations and eventually became quite prosperous. In Prokofiev's recollection, his father remains something of a background presence, always conscientious, a little unworldly *and forever concerned to avoid any friction with his superiors.*[43]

Impressions of his mother are warmer, and a lively picture of her emerges, uniformly positive and full of respect and admiration. Her encouragement and purposeful fostering of her son, largely at her own expense, were always very much present in the imagination of Prokofiev, who was proud of having been the centre of attention. Maria Grigoryevna Shitkova came from a family of small farmers and former serfs. Gifted in many ways, educated and involved in life, she contributed to the welfare of the local community. She organized the village school and taught at it herself. *When one reflects that concepts like enlightenment, progress, science and culture were prized by my parents above all else, then one can readily imagine that my mother derived great satisfaction from her teaching at the school.*[44]

Sergey Sergeyevich Prokofiev was his parents' third child, after the deaths of two infant daughters. They transferred all

their hopes and affections to their son. Prokofiev's intensely nostalgic description of his childhood in his autobiography may also have been partly due to the transformation of society in Russia at the time he was writing. In any event it seems certain that his childhood was remembered as an idyll, free of material cares and existential doubt. Here we may perhaps discover the basis for the composer's remarkable optimism and self-assurance, the twin pillars of his personality: *I was born in the year 1891. Borodin had been dead four years,*

The infant Prokofiev with his parents at Sontsovka in the Ukraine, 1892

Liszt *five*, Wagner *eight*, Mussorgsky *ten*. Tchaikovsky had two-and-a-half more years to live. He had completed his fifth symphony and not yet begun his sixth. In Russia Alexander III was on the throne. Lenin was twenty-one, Stalin just eleven years old.[45]

Country life on the estate provided Prokofiev with memorable first impressions: the Ukrainian landscape, the animals and plants, the rhythm of the seasons and the singing of folksongs. When playing with the peasant children it was always he who took on the role of leader. Music featured too among his earliest memories: *My mother was fond of music . . . She played the piano quite well and her languid existence in the country put her in a position to indulge this inclination as much as she wanted. One could scarcely say that she was musically talented. She found technique quite hard, and she was too shy to play before an audience. But she possessed three musical virtues: persistence, love and taste . . . At home I heard music from my earliest childhood.*[46] While his mother was playing, the three-year-old would take over the higher octaves on the piano and tinkled away freely in childish experimentation. Spontaneously and as yet with no knowledge of the notes, he came up with his own melodies, waltzes and marches, a polka, a rondo. Prokofiev designated a few bars of melody his mother had written down for him in the summer of 1896 as his earliest composition, giving it the eccentric title of *Indian Galop*, prompted by the much discussed plague and famine in India at the time: *The absent B flat should not be attributed to a preference for the Lydian mode. On the contrary, the young composer had not yet brought himself to include any of the black notes.*[47] *. . . One of his mother's sisters took all these scribblings with her to St Petersburg and handed them to a proficient copyist. After neat clean copies had been made, the pieces were bound together in an album with 'compositions by Seryoshenka Prokofiev' stamped in gold letters on the cover.*[48]

Prokofiev's education, however, was by no means solely confined to music. His intellectually inclined parents set great store by giving him as broad a general education as possible. Science and languages formed the core of the programme they organized. Prokofiev's diary

The game of Chess became one of Prokofiev's lifelong passions

also records a wide range of recreational activities, games as well as sports – croquet, riding, and walking on stilts, card games, and playing with tin soldiers and toy trains. He retained a passion for chess and bridge throughout his life. Besides all this he was involved not only in scientific and technical but also in literary pursuits. He wrote poems, including one called 'The Count' with his own illustrations. The young Prokofiev also delighted in his parents' extensive library. He was especially interested in *Granat's Encyclopaedia*, which after all *contained the flags of every nation, reproduced in colour.*[49]

From the winter of 1900 on, he was provided with a fund of new impressions by regular trips to Moscow.[50] His first theatrical experiences included Gounod's *Faust*, Borodin's *Prince Igor* and, at the Bolshoi Theatre, Tchaikovsky's *Sleeping Beauty*. Seeing these performances inspired Prokofiev to *produce plays himself. The plots were miserable and invariably included a swashbuckling duel. From an artistic point of view it was all Commedia dell'arte. We thought out the bare bones of the plot and then the actors improvised.*[51] He conceived of the idea of writing an opera: *The Giant, Music and Text. Act I, Scene I: Stenya, the daughter of our housekeeper, is seen sitting reading a book. Enter the giant. Stenya: 'Who can this be?' The giant: 'It's me.' The giant tries to seize her. A tremolo in the higher register with the right hand; with the left, descending fourths. Stenya has to scream very high notes, accompanied by the tremolo. Yegorka, another of the housekeeper's children, and I myself now enter. This stormy passage was invariably a success:*

"Stop! Wait! Look! Watch out!" I warn Yegorka, as the giant prepares to escape. Stenya faints away. The gallant knights lay her on the sofa. She sighs. They withdraw discreetly and just happen to drop their visiting cards. Stenya sings an aria:

Curtain. [52]

By the time he was admitted to the St Petersburg Conservatory three more operas had taken shape: *On Desert Islands, The Feast in Time of Plague* after Pushkin and *Undina* after a Russian version of the fairy-tale by de la Motte Fouqué. New scenic and musical elements appear, festive and battle music, waltzes and marches, all of it a mirror of the young composer's ever-widening repertoire of knowledge. Prokofiev remained addicted to the world of adventure and fairy-tale down to his very last works. The fantastic and the enchanted, stylization and defamiliarization, mask and play were to be his lifelong companions. Thus his predilection for certain plot motifs emerged from the very beginning, but also his detached attitude toward them.

A family acquaintance in Moscow, Yuri Pomeranzev, himself still a student at the Moscow Conservatory, later Director of the Bolshoi Theatre, managed to arrange an audition for Prokofiev with Sergey Taneyev. The long list of Prokofiev's childhood compositions impressed Taneyev, the city's highest musical authority at the time. Taneyev was a thoroughly competent technician, he regarded a foundation in harmony and the theory of composition as indispensable. On Taneyev's recommendation Reinhold Glière undertook to impart these systematically to the young composer. Glière had just left the Conservatory with the gold medal when he joined the secure and orderly Prokofiev household during the summer months of 1902 and 1903.[53] Here he gave daily piano and composition lessons, and he wrote the first of his own longer works. He praised Prokofiev for his thorough literary knowledge, his 'excellent memory, remarkable feeling for harmony . . . , bold and lively imagination . . . , and his extraordinary ability to invent figuratively apposite melodies . . . With him a serious, almost professional attitude to music and composing coexisted with many purely childish habits and delights.'[54]

Rheinhold Glière (1875–1956) was born in Kiev, where he was director of the conservatoire from 1914–1920, having taught both Prokofiev and Myaskovsky in the decade before. In 1905 he went to study in Berlin, having unwisely signed an anti-government petition, in the first flood of revolutionary fervour stimulated by the Russo-Japanese War. His *Second Symphony* was premièred in 1908 by Koussevitzky. Glière's revolutionary ballet *The Red Flower* was staged over two hundred times in the two years after its première in 1927. His career was extraordinarily long – he was conducting in Odessa in the month before he died in 1956. Although he studied in Moscow, with Arensky and Taneyev, his music is very much of the St Petersburg aesthetic, and is at its most successful in vignette form. His *Ballade for Cello and Piano* was very likely the inspiration for Prokofiev's own *Ballade*. His pupils also included Aram Khachaturian.

Glière brought order to Prokofiev's musical thinking with a remarkably skilful playfulness, while always keeping the individual development of the young composer in mind. He introduced him to the basic forms of music and guided him through the principles of instrumentation. One early orchestral piece was the storm music from the opera *On Desert Islands*. Prokofiev set not only lyrics by Pushkin and Lermontov but also his own texts to music. As regards larger forms he tested his wings with a *Piano Sonata*, a *Violin Sonata* and a *Symphony*. By September 1901 Prokofiev had already written an untitled piano piece, quite a long work with a dedication, in time for his father's name day. From this point on writing such pieces became something of a tradition, and Prokofiev with his knowledge of the *Lied* form called them 'little songs.' By 1906 he had composed five such song-cycles, each with twelve pieces, and always with personal dedications. Later, even beyond his time at the Conservatory, he repeatedly drew upon these early melodies. In this instance of recycling and utilizing material composed earlier we can see Prokofiev's immediate practical attitude to music – an attitude often apparent later (for instance in his resolute reshaping of all his stage and film music into suites for concert use).[55]

St Petersburg Conservatory

When the thirteen-year-old composer transferred to the Conservatory in St Petersburg in the autumn of 1904 his childhood came to an end. The conclusion of this period of secure personal and quiet artistic development coincided with the outbreak of political and social turmoil in Russia. A diary entry for November 1904 about the looming war with Japan represents Prokofiev's first recorded reaction to politics.[56]

The year 1905 began under the banner of the revolution. Young as I was, I had not noticed it approaching; that is, in the autumn I had more than once heard about strikes and disturbances, but not grasped what was really happening, and was inclined to see things in the light of the question, would father be coming to St Petersburg or not.[57] After the 'Bloody Sunday' massacre of 9 January, demands were being voiced even by composers for 'freedom of thought, conscience and speech', and for fundamental reforms to the 'tangled, abnormal conditions of Russian life',[58] as an open letter from Moscow musicians in the Moscow newspaper *Our Days* (*Nashi Dni*) expressed it. Prokofiev sent his father this account of the spread of the strikes to the Conservatories: *Just imagine! They have started to strike in the Conservatory. When I went to my harmony class today, I noticed that little groups had gathered everywhere, students of sixteen and seventeen shouting and making a lot of noise . . . But the main thing was that they had no objective at all.*[59] Understandably, Prokofiev later sought to justify this first reaction to revolutionary events as the attitude of a child: *It*

Russo–Japanese War 1904–5.
Triggered by a failure to seek diplomatic answers to rival territorial claims over expansion into Korea – by the Japanese – and into Manchuria – by the Russians. The first blow was struck by the Japanese, who torpedoed the Russian Pacific Fleet at Port Arthur. The size and power of the Japanese military was disastrously underestimated by the Russians as war on a massive scale ensued. The poor communications and vast distances of Russia sharply illustrated the incompetence of the Tsarist government and the campaign tottered towards the defeat of the Russians at Mukden. The shattering humiliation for the Russians was the naval Battle of Tsushima. The Russian Baltic Fleet had spent six months circumnavigating the globe, with the aim of relieving Port Arthur. The fleet was unequal to the modern Japanese fleet that lay waiting for them in the straits of Korea off the coast of Japan: the battle was over within hours, and all but three Russian ships were destroyed. News of the fall of Port Arthur precipitated the revolution of 1905.

shows the influence of discussions at home where I had been present and which I now naturally repeated. My mother's position was as follows: Since we had left my father behind in Sontsovka and moved to St Petersburg so that I could study music, the only imperative was that I should really study music and not let myself get involved in any shady business.[60]

In fact, the demands of the students aroused public attention not so much for their substance, which often took the form of very personal and to some extent banal proposals, but rather because of the support they received from a wide cross-section of the academic staff. More specifically, the question of whether Rimsky-Korsakov's appointment at the Conservatory should continue increasingly assumed a political dimension. An article in the Moscow journal *Russia* had led to Rimsky-Korsakov's suspension, quite unexpectedly in view of his international reputation as a composer and teacher. A storm of indignation and a wave of protest resignations followed. Glazunov, Lyadov, and a string of other professors left the institution as a mark of solidarity. A petition was issued from the ranks of the students, calling for the distribution of study notes and the suspension of teaching. Prokofiev also signed, after consulting with his mother. Eventually classes had to be cancelled altogether. The situation came to a head when striking students turned a production of Rimsky-Korsakov's opera *The Immortal Kashtchei* into an 'unprecedented, quite overwhelmingly powerful public demonstration'.[61] There was a general ban on all productions of his work.

Prokofiev's second year as a student continued unsettled, *the situation at the Conservatory remaining unresolved.*[62] In December the composer was celebrated as a symbol of resistance. There were clear signs of the imminent collapse of the revolutionary attempt to seize power. Reprisals, punitive expeditions and pogroms followed. The elderly Tolstoy tried, once again, to catch the public eye, proclaiming: 'I cannot remain silent'.[63] However, it was better to concede to the demands of the Conservatory students, with compromises. Rimsky-Korsakov, Lyadov and Glazunov returned, The latter as the elected Director. Normal teaching activities finally

Nikolay Rimsky-Korsakov (1844–1908) was born in Tikhivin. At twelve years of age he entered the St Petersburg Naval School. He was introduced to Balakirev, Borodin, Cui and Modest Mussorgsky by the critic Vladimir Stasov; together they formed the 'Mighty Handful'. He wrote most of his *First Symphony* whilst serving as a midshipman on the *Almaz*, and much of it whilst the warship was anchored off Gravesend in 1865. In 1875, he was engaged as professor of composition at the St Petersburg Conservatory. In 1905, he was briefly suspended from his post for supporting students agitating in support of the revolutionary movement. He taught Glazunov, Lyadov, Arensky, Ippalitov-Ivanov, Gretchaninov, Nikolay Tcherepnin and

Myaskovsky. Most famously, he taught the young Stravinsky. In 1907, he conducted concerts organized by Diaghilev in Paris.

resumed, and Prokofiev continued his studies. Conservatories generally had the reputation of being the custodians of ossified theories and structures. Lurking behind this view, along with the generational conflict, or youthful distrust of the acknowledged worthies of the time, was the romantic myth of original genius. Especially in Russia, where musical life had received its decisive impetus from dilettantes like Balakirev, Borodin and, Mussorgsky, it was easy for academically acquired knowledge to be neglected: *I . . .*

Anatoli Lyadov (1855–1914) was born in St Petersburg, where he studied at the Conservatory with Rimsky-Korsakov. He was expelled for failing to attend all of his classes, but upon re-admission graduated with great success, and by 1906 he was a professor of composition. With Lyapunov and Balakirev he collected folksongs for the Imperial Geographic Society, and he taught Prokofiev and Myaskovsky. He is most noted as a miniaturist; many of his smaller works are highly coloured evocations of Russian life, from the sounds of the Orthodox church to musical boxes.

at all events . . . never made the slightest connection between Lyadov's teaching and my own compositional plans. I continued to compose in my spare time and to enjoy it . . . I made no attempt to apply what I learned in my harmony course to my own composing. On the contrary, when I composed I tried to put all that behind me, and struggled to get back to roughly where I'd been two years before.[64]

The St Petersburg Conservatory was nevertheless a magnet for musically gifted young Russians. It owed its reputation to the fame of its teaching staff. The dominant figure was Rimsky-Korsakov. Now at the height of his fame, he had since 1871 been professor at the Conservatory which now bears his name. Opinion over Rimsky-Korsakov's importance in the history of music continues to be divided. His arrangements of Modest Mussorgsky's works especially come to mind.[65] It is claimed the elemental boldness of Mussorgsky's work has, sacrilegiously, been exposed to the tampering of 'a schoolmaster trapped in classicizing academic ideology'.[66] Rimsky-Korsakov was the only one from the circle of the 'Mighty Handful'[67] who had made an effort to familiarize himself with all aspects of compositional technique, as the disciples of Balakirev had to rid their music of 'European Academicism', as a moral and nationalistic issue, in direct conflict with what they saw as the Eurocentric Tchaikovsky and the Rubinsteins in Moscow. His breadth of education, his intellectual clarity and his scepticism were indeed truly academic. Rimsky-Korsakov's artistic presence spanned the entire century of Russian music thus far. The youngest member of the 'Five', he represented a direct link with the musical heritage of Glinka.[68] As the outstanding teacher of two generations of composers, including Glazunov and Lyadov, Stravinsky and Prokofiev, though this is still scarcely acknowledged, it is difficult to overestimate his role as one of the most versatile creative catalysts in the new music. His influence stretched well into the twentieth century.

Prokofiev's fellow student Boris Asafyev has left a description of Rimsky-Korsakov's teaching which is very reminiscent of Balakirev's idiosyncratic method. 'For hours Rimsky-Korsakov would go through every single piece of work with unflagging attention. All that was required of students was to catch the precious instructions and remarks, the telling judgements and advice . . . The pedagogical instructions repeatedly merged into a demonstration of the excellent Master's own artistry.'[69] Unlike Stravinsky, who had great admiration for his 'Master,' Prokofiev did not develop any special relationship with his teacher, even though he greatly admired his music for its concentration and compactness. He was also unable to make Rimsky-Korsakov's pedagogic methods work for him. *Even if Rimsky-Korsakov was the most interesting character of all the teachers at the Conservatory, his course was by no means the most interesting. This was because of the way he taught. As during the previous year, this time too he had a great many students, enough for two courses, whom he taught in sessions which lasted twice as long as normal, namely four hours without a break. It required formidable dedication to concentrate for the entire four hours.*[70]

There were differences of opinion and, not infrequently open conflicts with Lyadov, who gave courses in theory, counterpoint

'The Mighty Handful'. By the 19th century Western influences of polyphony and harmony were making an impression on Russian music. On the estates of the aristocracy music based on Italian and Austrian models found an enthusiastic reception. Western musical influences had also been introduced into the imperial chapel.

Mikhail Glinka (1804–1857) was the first composer to fuse these musical traditions. His *Life for the Tsar* is generally regarded as the first Russian opera, performed in St Petersburg in 1836. Glinka used a Russian theme and folk melodies in an Italian-style format.

Mili Balakirev (1836–1910) became the acknowledged leader of a school of composers concerned to create a distinctively Russian style of music. They included Alexander Borodin, César Cui, Modest Mussorgsky and Nikolay Rimsky-Korsakov. The critic Vladimir Stasov, the moving spirit behind the group, called them *moguchaia kuchka* the 'Mighty Handful'. Mussorgsky's orchestration and harmonies, considered unplayable at first, belied his remarkable talent. Of the 'handful', it is his and Rimsky-Korsakov's influence on future generations of musicians that proved the most long-lived.

and fugue. Many of Prokofiev's personal remarks regarded Lyadov's view of teaching as an *irksome duty,* [71] about his *complete indifference* [72] and lack of *interest in his students,*[73] his *grumbling and nagging* and his *hostile tone of voice,* [74] and mask a deeper mistrust between Prokofiev and his teacher. *About ten years later Asafyev confided to me how 'Lyadov once told me in passing, when speaking of you, that he found your music repellant, but that you were nonetheless talented and would develop your own mature style . . . And then he added: "But I don't understand why he comes to my classes; I say A to him, and he answers me with B".*[75]

Scoring and conducting were taught by Nikolay Tcherepnin, who was also in charge of the student orchestra. Tcherepnin, himself a student of Rimsky-Korsakov (and in 1909 conductor of *Les Ballets Russes* in Diaghilev's first Paris season), was a passionate devotee of everything new in music. *Of all my teachers Tcherepnin was the liveliest and most interesting musician, although he was a complete bundle of contradictions. His pronouncements on the future of music were no less interesting . . . At that time . . . he struck me as such a remarkable innovator that he completely turned my head.*[76]

Tcherepnin provided Prokofiev not only with an understanding of more recent European musical trends but also an introduction into radical Russian artistic movements. It was also he who kindled his interest in the music of the 18th century, in Haydn and Mozart, their transparency, lightness and directness.[77] This would later result in the composition of the Haydn-esque *First Symphony*.

In general, however, the programme at the Conservatory did not live up to the expectations of Prokofiev and especially not those of his mother. *Gradually my mother's dissatisfaction with the Conservatory increased, especially with regard to the core subject, composition. When I was sent to Moscow, everyone had vied to prove how interested he was. And when we first came to St Petersburg, Glazunov and Rimsky-Korsakov had also shown me unusual attention. When I entered the Conservatory however, everything lapsed into indifference and superficiality.*[78] He repeatedly adopted the judgements of his ambitious mother. She was uneasy and impatient at the regulated pace of a thorough programme of study, which covered everything from general theory and harmony, through courses in counterpoint and fugue, genre studies, down to scoring and instrumentation. But one can also assume that Prokofiev had his personal problems, especially in a new social environment and given the age differential. His difficulties are mentioned in the reminiscences of a contemporary fellow student, Vera Alpers, who remained a lifelong friend: 'His extreme and hurtful opinions, his fanatical commitment to the truth and his inability to avoid dangerous confrontations did not endear him to those who found themselves exposed to his critical sallies. During lessons in Lyadov's

Nikolay Tcherepnin (1873–1945) was born in St Petersburg, where Prokofiev studied conducting with him. Like Prokofiev, he was also a student of Rimsky-Korsakov in the late 1890s. In 1909, he conducted the inaugural season of Diaghilev's *Ballets Russes* in Paris. He was the founder of a family dynasty of innovative composers; the radical American composer and musical inventor Gloria Coates studied with his son Alexander, who completed Mussorgsky's *The Marriage* in the late 1930s. He died in Paris, where he was the director of the Russian Conservatory until his death.

class for example, he would carefully take note of the mistakes made by his fellow students in their harmony homework, even entering them systematically in a book at home, for which he earned strenuous protestations from his classmates. However, the harshness of his views, his habit of stirring, his contentious spirit, and his insistent questioning of authorities did not prove an obstacle to his distinguishing himself in Conservatory circles by his outstanding ability, thirst for knowledge and quick reactions, as well as by an astounding sense of humour.'[79]

Prokofiev formed a lifelong and consistently close friendship with Nikolay Myaskovsky, who with his twenty-seven symphonies later became the first Soviet symphonist of rank. Myaskovsky had made a belated decision to exchange his career as an engineer in the army for that of a professional musician. In 1906, still an officer, he entered Lyadov's class. Typically the fifteen-year-old Prokofiev found his equal in a discussion partner ten years older than himself. Yet he also discovered in this thoughtful and modest friend, devoid of all exalted notions, inclined to self-doubt and melancholy, a counterweight to his own self-absorbed and wilful personality. For all their differences in temperament, Myaskovsky's opinion was always his primary, critical yardstick. Their intensive correspondence continued until Myaskovsky's death in 1950, reflecting the constructive nature of this interchange.[80]

One joint venture they agreed upon in the summer of 1908 was the composition of a symphony. But the aesthetic premises on which this plan was to proceed proved to be at variance: *I am frankly astounded at your spinning things out to one hundred and twenty pages . . . What could be more deadly than a long symphony? In my opinion a symphony should ideally last twenty*

Prokofiev as a student, in front of Mozart's bust at the Moscow Conservatory

Alexander Glazunov (1865–1936) was born in St Petersburg. A child prodigy, he began lessons with Rimsky-Korsakov when he was fifteen years old, and his *First Symphony* was premièred by Balakirev a few years later. He was elected as Director of the St Petersburg Conservatory in 1905, having resigned nine months earlier in protest at the dismissal of Rimsky-Korsakov. Whilst there he refused to prevent the illegal registration of Jewish students, who were not even allowed to be in the capital, enabling the great pedagogue and soloist Leopold Auer to produce a stream of virtuosi including Jascha Heifetz. Glazunov was heard to remark that non-Jewish students were 'disappoint-

ingly Christian'. Auer premièred his wonderful *A minor Concerto* in 1905. Glazunov left Russia in 1928, exhausted by the political turmoil of the years after the Revolution.

minutes, or thirty at most, and in my symphony I have striven for maximum concentration: any suggestion of long-windedness I ruthlessly cross out.[81] Even the performance of Prokofiev's *Symphony in E Minor* – thanks to a recommendation by Glazunov it was taken on by the court orchestra for a closed rehearsal – proved something of a disillusioning experience: *The instrumentation of the symphony was too insignificant and left a rather flat impression.*[82]

In the spring of 1909 Prokofiev sat for his final examination. Lyadov found fault with the exuberance of his *Sixth Piano Sonata*: 'They all want to become Skryabins!'[83] Josef Witol, Prokofiev's instructor in musical form, likewise judged the eighteen-year-old composer 'a radical innovator to the point of extremes, with rather one-sidedly developed technique'.[84] The verdict on the work he submitted, which included the final scene from *The Feast in Time of Plague*, was overwhelmingly negative. Even his piano playing aroused only partial admiration. Interestingly enough, Prokofiev

FINAL EXAM

Anna Esipova (1855–1914). The pianist Anna Esipova was one of the most distinguished students of Leschetizky, to whom she was married from 1880 to 1892. She was famous for the furious intensity of her touring, by the standards of her time, always giving more than fifty concerts a year whilst she was active as a performer. She taught in St Petersburg from 1893 to 1908.

had chosen the arrangement of a fugue for organ by Buxtehude as part of his examination. 'His technical grounding,' according to Glazunov, was 'quite brilliant. His performance is unusual, original but not always governed by artistic taste.'[85] And even Glière, after Prokofiev had called on him in Moscow, commented on his former pupil with detachment: 'He has become very self-assured; his judgement of contemporary music is emphatically "left of centre". He is ready to dethrone any generally acknowledged authority you care to name. Despite this, we parted friends.'[86]

After his exams at the Conservatory, Prokofiev stayed on for another five years, and consolidated his interpretational skills. He continued to study conducting with Tcherepnin, but now took piano lessons with the internationally acclaimed pianist Anna Esipova whilst attending the opera school. Thus, notwithstanding his less than brilliant grades, Prokofiev was now indisputably, in official jargon, a 'Free Artist'.

St Petersburg: Laboratory of Modernism [87]

The year 1909 marked the beginning of the 'historical Avant-garde movement'.[89] Filippo Marinetti published the Futurist Manifesto in the Paris newspaper *Le Figaro*,[90] Sergey Diaghilev began the first season of *Ballets Russes* in Paris, Wassily Kandinsky completed the transition to the first truly abstract painting. In music Alexander Skryabin propounded the notion of a 'tone centre' as the new harmonic and melodic principle of construction in his works. And Arnold Schoenberg with his piano pieces Op 11 and his cycle of Stefan George songs Op 15 attempted, as he put it, to break through 'all the bounds of an outmoded aesthetic'.[91]

St Petersburg, the political capital, was the cultural and spiritual centre of Russia on the threshold of the modern era, integrated, far more so than Moscow, into the system of European cultural activity. Alongside the influential 'Imperial Russian Music Society' sponsored by the government, and the concerts of the publisher Belayev and other conservative and nationally oriented musical societies, from 1903 onwards Alexander Siloti was giving his inspiring concerts. It was here that the international conductors, virtuosos, and singers met, and here too that the new Western music of Reger and Strauss, Ravel

St Petersburg by F Alexeyev, 1794

and Debussy first made an impact. What counted more even than the appointment of Siloti in the development of modern music in Russia were the activities of the innumerable small musical gatherings and private circles. Starting in 1901, the music critic Viatcheslav Karatygin, together with Walter Nouvel and Alfred Nurok, both music lovers and professional civil servants, organized a series of 'Evenings of Contemporary Music'. In many ways these were a continuation of the tradition of Belayev's *'Les Vendredis'. They all had decided tastes and a sharp tongue. They would meet on Thursdays in the dimly lit warehouse of the Bekker piano manufacturers and play new compositions through, selecting the most interesting from which they could then arrange a few evenings of chamber music during the season. I don't know how these concerts survived – they did not make a great splash, they were given in a small hall, and the entrance cost, I believe, thirty kopecks. But all the critics were present, as was everyone who was interested in modern music.*[92] These 'Evenings' came within the orbit of the 'World of Art' association of artists and the arts bulletin of the same name. This movement, initiated by Diaghilev and Alexander Benois and also shaped by artists such as Léon Bakst and Anna Ostroumova-Lebedeva, pursued a two-fold objective: to spread Western European modernism in Russia, and to establish a progressive Russian artistic movement of international standing but with its own distinctive national imprint. Prokofiev's teacher Nikolay Tcherepnin was also closely associated with this group, and conducted the first season of *Les Ballets Russes* in Paris in 1909. Under the auspices of the 'Evenings of contemporary Music' the Russian first performances of works by Schoenberg and above all by French modernist composers took place; Debussy, Paul Dukas, Florent Schmitt, Ravel. Myaskovsky, Stravinsky, and Prokofiev also entered the lists with their own compositions for the first time here.

On 18 December 1908 Prokofiev played seven of his piano pieces: *Fairy-Tale* (later included under Op 3), *Snow Flakes* (reworked for *War and Peace*), *Souvenirs, Élan, Despair, Suggestion Diabolique* (all in *Four*

Pieces for Piano Op 4) and *Prayer*. Prokofiev's pretentious titles point to his unorthodox compositional idiom. What is fascinating about these pieces is the relentless rhythmic vehemence that Prokofiev sought to fully integrate with the tonal elements of his music. The composer's distrust of traditional

Prokofiev at the piano at Nikopol, 1910

conceptions of piano music surfaces, his suspicion of the organic fusion of Chopin's melody, harmony, and rhythm, or Debussy's refined mood-painting, but also his wariness of the metaphysical excesses of Skryabin's works. Myaskovsky considered 'the complete absence of any indistinctness in the articulation, the clear free-flowing form, the terse almost aphoristic impressiveness and characteristic plasticity of the themes, the precise lively rhythm' as among the 'extraordinarily valuable qualities'[93] of this music. It was no doubt Prokofiev's performance of the *Suggestion Diabolique* that left the most memorable impression: relentless, aggressive ostinati, harsh tonal tensions, hammering percussive chords at high speed, headlong dissonant staccati, crass contrasts of dynamic, and heavily accented rhythms, all this was played with a *dry, robust touch*.[94]

Prokofiev, while still a student at the Conservatory, suddenly found himself on an equal footing with the most advanced composers. First of all press reports appeared:[95] 'This young composer belongs to the extreme wing of the Modernists and goes far beyond the contemporary French in boldness and originality.'[96] Karatygin declared Prokofiev the antithesis of Skryabin. Suddenly the high-flown spirituality of the idol of the Symbolist avant-garde seemed stale. The significance of Prokofiev's appearances at these 'Evenings' can scarcely be overestimated. Even more than his graduation from the Conservatory it marked a new departure in the 'Free Artist's' life. In February 1910 Prokofiev's début in Moscow

THE ANTITHESIS OF SKRYABIN

Synaesthesia. In his directions for *Die Glückiche Hand*, Arnold Schoenberg required a 'crescendo of illumination'. This is a clear indication of Synaesthesia. This term, first used in the modern sense by Jules Millet in 1892, is the experience whereby a stimulus applied to one sense elicits a response from another. Isaac Newton is said to have inculcated the division of the visible spectrum into seven degrees by direct analogy with the diatonic division of the musical scale into seven degrees. Naturally, Synaesthesia occurs through all art, and particularly poetry, but was especially popular with the symbolist poets, such as Baudelaire, particularly in his sonnet 'Correspondances', mainly because the drugged or disturbed claimed to have experienced it. Baudelaire, himself heavily influenced by Thomas de Quincey's *Confessions of an English Opium Eater* wrote: *Les Parfums, les Couleurs, et les Sens se répondent*. In music, Synaesthesia is closely linked to the old, highly subjective association of certain notes and tonalities with other sensory phenomena or emotions. In the early twentieth century, it was most closely associated with the ambitious schemes and wild imaginings of Skryabin, whose score for *Prometheus* included very precise notations of light effects, represented on a stave in the manner of an instrumental line. The concept was always confused by its unfortunate subjectivity, whilst most composers 'see' C major as a 'white' key, there all correspondence ends, Rimsky-Korsakov saw the 'dark' key of F sharp as dull green, whereas Skryabin saw it as bright blue.

followed, and shortly after that his first appearance in a public symphony concert. The composer embarked on writing longer works, remarkably enough in the traditional Italian genres of sonata, concerto, symphony and opera. For the first time his compositions were printed, and also furnished with opus numbers.

The year 1910 also saw the death of his father. Prokofiev was now responsible for his own finances and faced a break with the past in his private life. Compositionally Prokofiev tried to deal with the experience of the death of his father in the symphonic 'painting' *Autumn Sketches*. It is an elegiac piece, wholly trapped in the romantic world outlook. *The critics wrote about soft rain, about falling leaves, and they quoted poems. But not one of them discovered that an inner world is reflected here and not an outer one, and that an 'autumn' of that kind can come in spring and summer.*[97] The preceding orchestral work, called *Dreams*, is also dark and melancholy. Prokofiev dedicated it to Skryabin, with whose work *Reverie* it is clearly linked. Prokofiev's orchestral music was as yet still a long way from the boldness and exuberance of his aphoristic piano compositions. In 1909, even before the tone poems, he wrote the *Sinfonietta*, five miniatures, simple in structure, transparent in their orchestration, and clear in cadence. Prokofiev revised the *Sinfonietta* several times, and it is clear that he valued it highly, as he eventually reissued it as Op 48. In *World of Art* circles knowledge and transmission of the classics was taken for granted. For Prokofiev, thanks to the mediation of his teacher Tcherepnin (to whom the *Sinfonietta* is dedicated), it provided an escape from worn-out pathos and fulfilled his more avant-garde aspirations.

In 1911 Prokofiev succeeded for the first time in getting one of his compositions published. The previous year, at the beginning of his public career, he had failed to kindle the interest of publishers. Initially Sergey Koussevitzky's interest in everything new in music, which later in Europe and the United States would enable him to become Prokofiev's key patron too, had to contend with the veto of a publishing committee. *Rakhmaninov and Medtner . . . roundly rejected anything that displayed even the slightest hint of more modern music.*[98]

The publishing house Bessel also responded negatively. *Jurgenson replied to me that he was inundated with manuscripts and had no time to look over work by young composers.*[99] But after an endorsement from the musicologist Alexander Ossovsky and a recommendation by Taneyev, Jurgenson relented, and took on four of Prokofiev's works: the *First Piano Sonata* Op 1 and a selection of piano pieces which appeared as Op 2, 3, and 4. Because of printing costs, Jurgenson published exclusively piano pieces (later putting out Op 12 and 16 and eventually also the *First Piano Concerto*). He remained Prokofiev's sole publisher until 1919.

The composer's attempts to get his work performed came to nothing at first. In July 1911 Prokofiev managed to have his

Prokofiev *Ballade*. In 1902, Prokofiev began work on a work suggested by Reinhold Glière. *Back at home, I settled down to write the violin sonata that Glière had suggested to me. Special music paper had been bought for the purpose. I remember that this sonata marked a great step forward. I used the main theme of the 1st movement for my 'Ballade for Cello and Piano' Op 15.*

In 1916, Siloti presented the first whole concert of music by Prokofiev. The programme included *Sarcasmes*, the Op 25 Sonata, Toccata, the Scherzo for Bassoon, and a major new work, *Ballade for Cello and Piano*.

Medtner and Rakhmaninov were both at the concert. They were not impressed, and reserved particular opprobrium for the *Ballade*. Medtner's response was unequivocal: 'if that is music, then I am no musician.' Myaskovsky, on the other hand, commented 'it seems as if it had been written especially for Casals.' Myaskovsky's remark was very perceptive. Siloti had brought Casals to play at his concert series shortly before the work was composed. At this time Casals was revolutionizing cello playing. Not until the arrival of Prokofiev's last great collaborator, Rostropovich, would cello playing take such a leap into the future again.

orchestral pieces *Dreams* and *Autumnal Sketches* included in a programme of summer concerts in Sokolniki Park. He remained excluded from the academic concert halls. But he was now catching the eye of critics: 'I don't think these young fledgling musical birds deserve quite so much space and attention – all of twice in one season. It would be much better for them to wait. As regards talent, Mr Prokofiev comes close to Kalinnikov; I believe he could write as well too, if like Borodin and other St Petersburg musicians he were more straightforward. But he goes in for grimacing and is determined to be a modernist, and modernism doesn't suit him.'[100] Prokofiev's friend Myaskovsky defended him staunchly: 'He was rejected by you, but as regards talent and independent-mindedness I would make so bold as to rate him higher than Stravinsky. Admittedly he lacks the latter's staggering technique, but that is a matter of practice, and Prokofiev's ability to express himself in his own idiom is undoubtedly more highly developed.'[101] At the 'Evenings of Contemporary Music' Prokofiev remained on the programme.

With his work at the Conservatory's opera studio, plans for new operas were also ripening. Once again the composer first reverted to a work from his childhood, the *The Feast in Time of Plague*. He now sought to capture Pushkin's poetic meaning by counterpointing the bacchanalian scenes against the scenes of death. Prokofiev's first original work for the theatre is *Maddalena*, composed in 1911. This opera was based on a melodrama by Baroness Lieven, the pseudonym of a young society lady, *who was more agreeable in company than talented as a dramatist.*[102] Adapting elements from Oscar Wilde's *Florentine Tragedy*, the piece describes the fateful love conflict of two aristocrats at the time of the Renaissance. Prokofiev's dense declamatory style, full of expressive effects, conceived as a dramatic unity, of course made excessive demands on the Conservatory's resources. The opera could not be produced. Once more it was Myaskovsky who publicized his friend's work in aptly chosen words: 'One senses how much his talent has developed lately. Apart from his quite unusual and at times – in terms of freshness and uncanny power – astonishing harmonic boldness, it is his volcanic explosiveness of temperament that most surprises one. In its intensity of expression the opera is reminiscent of Richard Strauss, except that it lacks his lyrical banalities.'[103]

Concurrently with work on the opera, Prokofiev was also writing his *First Piano Concerto*, in his own estimation his first more or less mature work, in as much as it uses new sound configurations and formal innovations: *Firstly in regard to new sound combinations of piano and orchestra; then formally in a repetition of the sonata allegros next to the introduction after the exposition and at the end, then in the short andante which has crept in before the transition, and finally as a scherzo in the transition itself and at the beginning of the recapitulation in the guise of a cadenza. Certainly one can object that using this form the concerto turns into a series of single episodes; but these episodes were quite closely related to one another. The implementation of the idea was better than in the earlier scores.*[104] Strongly self-assertive in the motoring double octaves of the introduction, full of energy and power, masterly in bringing the single movement form to life, this terse and astringent work perfectly reflects the composer's state of mind at the time of its inception. The reactions of audience and critics to the concerto, both positive and negative, at the Moscow and St Petersburg premières were intense. They confirmed the composer's growing reputation and, as he had calculated, his role as the *enfant terrible* of Russian music. It was this work that Prokofiev played in 1914 after his final year at the Conservatory, the last year of peace in old Russia, in his last concert under Tcherepnin (Prokofiev received the Conservatory's Anton Rubinstein prize for piano and, as one of the perks, a grand piano from Schröder, the piano manufacturers); and again the same year in a subscription concert under Koussevitzky.

The first performance of the *Second Piano Concerto* caused a furore. In its harshening of the harmonies and quest for new ways of increasing the virtuoso element, the work shows the composer's uncompromising search for originality and rejection of all forms of imitation. The press response was correspondingly divided. *Karatygin wrote a flattering article, others made fun of me. In the supplement to the 'St Petersburg News' they wrote: 'Onto the podium steps a young man with the face of a St Petersburg schoolboy, S. Prokofiev. He seats himself at the piano and begins now wiping, now trying out the keys, checking which sound higher and which lower, and all this with a dry sharp touch. The audience are restive. Some get excited, others stand up and rush toward the exit: "Music like this can drive a person mad!" The hall empties. With a mercilessly dissonant chord from the brass, the concerto breaks off.'*[105] The audience was shocked exactly in the way the composer had imagined, but the scandalous première led to his unqualified acceptance in Russian modernist circles. Prokofiev's compositions now appeared on concert programmes more and more frequently. Offers from publishers piled up. His name became familiar in St Petersburg salons and theatre circles. Diaghilev began to show an interest in him.

In 1913 Prokofiev had already made a trip to Paris, the fountain-head of modernism in all the arts. Diaghilev had celebrated a succession of triumphs in his self-appointed mission of transmitting Russian culture to Western Europe. He began with exhibitions of Russian painting and sculpture before moving on to promote concerts and opera productions. The legendary performance of *Boris Godunov* with Fyodor Chaliapin in 1908 was a spectacular success. He finally concentrated wholly on *Les Ballets Russes*. Diaghilev managed to control and coordinate some of the outstanding artistic personalities of literature, painting, music, and dance of the time: Cocteau and Bakst, Matisse and Picasso, Debussy and Ravel, Stravinsky and Prokofiev, Nijinsky, Lifar and Pavlova, Massine and Balanchine. For twenty years the premières of *Les Ballets Russes* became the focal point of aesthetic developments in Europe. Prokofiev had missed the scandalous première of Stravinsky's *The Rite of Spring* by a few days. But he was in time to hear *Petrushka*, Ravel's *Daphnis and Chloé* and Florent Schmitt's *Tragedy of Salome*.

In the summer of 1914, after finishing at the Conservatory and only a few days before the assassination of Archduke Franz Ferdinand at Sarajevo, Prokofiev went abroad again. He wanted to attend *Les Ballets Russes* London season, which featured some of Diaghilev's most impressive productions.[106] His mother gave him the

Diaghilev and his nurse, portrait by Léon Bakst, 1904

trip as a reward for the successful completion of his studies.[107] *This season was indeed interesting: Chaliapin was singing, Richard Strauss conducting, and many novel items appeared too. Diaghilev himself made a great impression in his top hat and tails, monocle and white gloves.*[108] No doubt

Massine, Goncharova, Larionov, Stravinsky and Bakst, collaborators in *Les Ballets Russes*

Diaghilev's fashion sense appealed to Prokofiev whose own wardrobe was noted for its flamboyance.

Prokofiev's own ideas of course revolved wholly around opera. He thought ballet music was not serious enough, but rather easy and devoid of substance. Prokofiev moreover always conceived of his operas without any concrete sense of what their production might entail. His disagreements over ballet, by contrast, were related throughout his life to actual commissions. So these works, adjusted as they are to the aesthetic of each commissioning authority, also depict more accurately than others the biographically determined shifts in emphasis in the composer's work as a whole:[109] *Ala and Lolli, The Buffoon, Pas D'Acier* and *The Prodigal Son* reflect the changes inherent in Diaghilev's aesthetic premises; the acrobatic ballet *Trapeze* was composed as an occasional piece for a small touring ensemble, in the case of *On the Banks of Dnieper* Serge Lifar tried to repeat the success of *The Prodigal Son*, while in Prokofiev's Soviet ballets *Romeo and Juliet, Cinderella* and *The Stone Flower* one can recognize the constraints of socialist realism.

With his ideas on opera, particularly his plan for an opera based on Dostoevsky, Prokofiev could get no response from Diaghilev. Diaghilev remained convinced that this genre was in decline: 'Opera is passé, today people want ballet and pantomime.'[110] *When Nouvel introduced me to him, he immediately started talking about ballet. I tried to talk about opera and about 'The Gambler' but nothing came of it. With 'Maddalena', he didn't like the subject.*[111] Diaghilev showed an interest in the *Second Piano Concerto*, and *hit upon the curious idea that perhaps one might adapt the piece for the theatre.*[112] But putting the idea into practice then proved difficult. Prokofiev received the commission for a new ballet. Sergey Gorodetsky, in the throes of transforming himself from a Symbolist to an Acmeist, undertook to write a scenario on a topic from pre-Christian Slav mythology. And Prokofiev set to work on the music for the ballet *Ala and Lolli,* possibly in an attempt to evoke the success of Stravinsky's *Le Sacre du Printemps* and *Les Noces.*

Everything was so interesting in London that I didn't notice the approach of war and only by chance was able to get back to St Petersburg a few days before it broke out.[113] It is difficult to tell whether Prokofiev's account of his own lack of political involvement at this time is merely evidence of genuine unconcern. In the Stalinist Russia of the 1940s the composer would have needed to account for his sojourn abroad during this decisive phase of the revolutionary Soviet state. Myaskovsky, as an officer, was enlisted whereas Prokofiev, as the only son of a widow, became a reservist. Together with his mother he left the Tsarist capital (which after the German declaration of war was Slavicized as 'Petrograd'). Once out in the Caucasus, which was as remote as it was peaceful, it was only through Myaskovsky's letters that he came to hear of world events.

More important than the war, more important even than his other projects – for instance, the revision of the *Sinfonietta* for one of Siloti's concerts and music for Hans Christian Andersen's fairy-tale *The Ugly Duckling* – was his work on the ballet *Ala and Lolli* for Diaghilev. Prokofiev had high hopes for this work. However, it would be another seven years before the first production of one of his ballets by Diaghilev. *Gorodetsky had dug out a few suitable Scythian characters, but couldn't come up with any ideas for the drama, and it took us many meetings to get a plot together . . . As I received the outline scene by scene, I immediately wrote up the music. I was after something larger. I had already heard Stravinsky's 'The Rite of Spring' in concert, but had not understood it. Probably I was seeking something similar for myself.*[114] The idea of archaic dances and pagan blood cults, of sun worship and fertility rites, must have appealed strongly to Prokofiev's notions of what modernism in music should be all about. Here barbarous

Alexander Siloti (1863–1945) was born in the industrial town of Kharkov. He studied composition with Tchaikovsky's associate and ally, Nicolai Rubinstein at the Moscow Conservatory, with Liszt for three years from 1883, and later became an influential piano teacher in Moscow. Rakhmaninov, his cousin, was his most famous pupil. From 1903 he was instrumental in organizing orchestras and concert series in St Petersburg, and he invited Casals, Mengelburg, and Chaliapin to perform for him. It was at one of these concerts that Prokofiev heard the Catalan cellist, whose playing had a great impact on his writing for the instrument. In 1916, Siloti presented the first all-Prokofiev concert.

dissonances and sharp contrasts fell into place, as did harsh melodies, jagged harmonies, shrill sound effects and the emphasis on rhythm. But of course an apparent imitation of *The Rite of Spring*, coming only a year after the première of Stravinsky's ballet, could scarcely have struck Diaghilev as timely. *Nurok and Nouvel came and listened to me but said nothing, and Nouvel wrote to Diaghilev that I was engaged in a lot of nonsense over nonsensical material. Diaghilev asked me to come to Italy, where he happened to be at the time, promising to organize a concert for me in Rome and to pay for the journey.*[115]

In Rome, Prokofiev played his *Second Piano Concerto*, with mixed results. Leonide Massine, Diaghilev's choreographer during these years, praised the 'unique combination of youthful exuberance and Russian intensity'.[116] The composer was not, however, able to repeat the sensation of its first performance in this his first concert appearance in Western Europe.

'Dear Igor,' Diaghilev wrote to Stravinsky, 'a string of new questions: but first Prokofiev. Yesterday he played at the Augusteum, with some success. But that's not the main thing. He brought me a ballet. The draft is a St Petersburg hodgepodge, good for a Mariinsky Theatre production ten years ago. As he says himself, the score is "pure music, avoiding all 'Russianisms' as far as possible." And that's just the point: pure music, and pretty bad music at that, so we've got to start from scratch . . . Prokofiev is gifted, but what can one expect from him when the most cultivated person he associates with is Gorodetsky,[117] who only confuses him with his ideas. Prokofiev is easily influenced, and he seems to me more affable than one might suspect from his initial arrogance. I will bring the piece round to you; it has to be completely altered, otherwise we can never put it on.'[118]

Diaghilev showed Prokofiev round Italy – Rome, Milan, Naples, Palermo, Sorrento, and Pompei. He introduced the composer to Italian artists, among them Marinetti, and enabled him to get to know Stravinsky better. And he commissioned Prokofiev to compose another ballet: *The Buffoon* (*Le Chout*) based on Alexander Afanasiev's collection of Russian folk tales. *This time Diaghilev signed a proper contract with me for over three thousand roubles.* 'Now you must write music that is truly Russian.'[119]

Meanwhile Prokofiev's enthusiasm for opera continued to leave Diaghilev unimpressed. In the autumn of 1915 the composer set to work on his long-cherished plan for a Dostoevsky opera. Many theatres were experimenting with stage adaptations of Dostoevsky's novels at the time. Myaskovsky had turned to *The Idiot*, and Prokofiev took on *The Gambler*. He redrafted the text of the novella as an anti-realistic grotesque in four acts which lacked the final liberation of the original ending.

Prokofiev explained his project in two interviews.[120] Fascinated by Dostoevsky's language, he placed the dialogues at the centre of his opera, sticking substantially to the original text. *In this particular case, Dostoevsky's prose is clearer, more graphic and convincing than any made-up lines.*[121] The opera is composed as recitative, without arias, ensembles, and choruses. Thus the musical development of the characters is to a high degree determined by what is happening on stage, in line with Meyerhold's theatrical notions of

Sergey Lifar, Diaghilev and Stravinsky

the abiding importance of plot and the avoidance of all static set pieces. Prokofiev's music is ignited by the dynamic development of the fictional intrigue: harsh, free-tonal harmonic series with virtuoso descriptive orchestration, declamatory melodic contours on the acknowledged model of Mussorgsky's one-act Gogol opera *The Wedding*, closely tailored to the intonations of the text. At the Mariinsky Theatre in Petrograd Meyerhold supported the work, and Prokofiev tried to arrange a production at the Moscow Bolshoi Theatre. But the Revolution put an end to all such plans. Ten years later the composer returned to the score, completing and reworking it, again in close collaboration with Meyerhold. This time the planned production at the Leningrad Academy's opera house had to contend with aggressive protests from the Russian Association of Proletarian Musicians (RAPM). In 1929 *The Gambler* was finally produced in French at the Royal Theatre in Brussels. It was the only production during the composer's lifetime.

Prokofiev rearranged the music for the ballet *Ala and Lolli* into the *Scythian Suite*. It was the first of many suites that the composer would put together from the music he had written for ballet, opera, theatre, and film, and it secured the popularity and wider currency of his music. The first performance of the *Scythian Suite* in one of Siloti's concerts on 16 January 1916 created a sensation. Outrage and enthusiasm were displayed in equal measure. *After the Suite the same uproarious noise broke out in the hall as after the first performance of the 'Second Piano Concerto' in Pavlovsk, except that the entire music world of Petrograd was represented here. Glazunov, whom I had personally invited to the concert, lost control for a second time, and, appalled by the sunrise sequence, stormed out of the hall eight beats before the end. The newspapers observed that 'the expletives the Director of the Conservatory let out about the new work were not the most considered.' The man on the timpani had beaten through the hide of his instrument, and Siloti promised to send it to me as a souvenir.*[122] A second performance of this suite was scheduled by Koussevitzky for 12 December but cancelled because a number of the musicians were called up for military service. Even so, the redoubtable critic Sabanayev saw fit to write an outright condemnation of this 'barbarous'[123] music.

With the *Classical Symphony* Prokofiev tried to distance himself no less sharply from the expressive idiom of late Romanticism, while operating on quite a different plane from the explosive power and aggressiveness of the *Scythian Suite*. This work has been heralded as a forerunner of the neo-classicism that permeated all the arts in the period between the two world wars. The composer himself repeatedly rejected the notion of imitating traditional styles and traditional techniques, *Bach-isms and false notes*,[124] as he put it. He thought of his symphony as an experiment, both in style and compositional method; this was the first major composition that he wrote away from the piano. *I was intrigued by the idea of making an entire symphonic piece without the piano. A composition written this way would probably have more transparent orchestral colours.*[125] He had been introduced to the idea of a Haydn-esque work by his teacher Tcherepnin. *If Haydn were still alive today, I thought, he would retain his own mode of writing but also assimilate a few new things. That's the kind of symphony I wanted to write – a symphony in the classical style.*[126] Prokofiev's own classicism was little more than an interlude, although he returned to the language of the 'Classical' symphony in his 1948 sonata for solo violin. Nevertheless the composer repeatedly reverted to such stylistic features as transparency of orchestration and clarity of form, albeit with an underlying tone of genial irony.

In his vocal compositions Prokofiev remained under the spell of Symbolism for much longer. Prokofiev's sensitivity to the sound structures of the Russian language is reflected in the almost total absence of vocal music from his work during the years spent abroad. Evidently familiarity with a foreign language could not inspire the composer to write songs.

It was Konstantin Balmont whose lyrics, so rich in striking

sound effects, most influenced Prokofiev's work over an extended period. The poet is as much present in Prokofiev's first choral works, *Two Choral Pieces for Female Voice* Op 7, as in the cantata[127] *Seven, They are Seven*, the main work produced during the year of the Revolution, and in many of his songs from Op 9 to Op 36. Balmont also inspired the title for the *Twenty Piano Pieces* Op 22: *Visions fugitives*.

Cinq Melodies. The *Five Songs without Words*, Op 35 for voice and piano, were premièred by Nina Koshets on 27 March 1921. Prokofiev wrote, *Nina Koshets prayed with her head on my shoulder that heaven would send me even a drop of love for her. She must be a great singer because heaven has so far turned a deaf ear to her prayers and she is leaving tomorrow.*

In 1920, Prokofiev helped her to leave Russia via Constantinople. He introduced her to his American manager and sent her some characteristically acerbic advice before she arrived in the United States. *For America, you must write your surname with an E not an I, since if you write it with an I, it will evoke undesirable associations.*

Koussevitzky toured her as 'Chaliapin in Petticoats'. By the 1930s she was doing dubbing work in Hollywood; finally she became a restaurateuse.

Prokofiev spent more than half the year 1917, between the events of February and October, away from revolutionary Petrograd, and composed far more than usual. He completed the *First Violin Concerto*, the *Classical Symphony* and the *Visions fugitives*. Besides the 'Chaldaic Oath', *Seven, They are Seven* he also wrote the *Third* and *Fourth Piano Sonatas*, as well as concertos, sonatas, symphonies – all traditional genres, pure music. Later in his autobiography Prokofiev endeavoured, almost as an obligatory gesture, to claim the cantata at least, as one work which represented a fitting response to the spirit of the Revolution. *The events of the Revolution which were stirring Russia forced their way into my sub-conscious and demanded to be given shape. It was not clear to me, however, how this might come about, and strangely my attention turned toward remote antiquity in search of a subject. The fact that the thoughts and feelings of those times had survived so many millennia captured my imagination. A suitable subject presented itself in the Chaldaic oath chiselled in cuneiform lettering into the walls of an Arcadian temple, which had been put into verse by Winkler and by Balmont.*[128] It is a work of extremely expressionistic character, and as such linked to the adjacent operas *Maddalena* and *The Fiery Angel*. Its return to an archaic theme also establishes its connection with the *Scythian Suite*. The text underlying this work, however, is less concerned with liberation and the joys of life than chaos and destruction. Precisely because this is what this 'decadent' mythic text conveys, and even though it was the first of Prokofiev's scores to be published in the Soviet Union, it was never performed there.

Prokofiev in Petrograd, 1916

Prokofiev's retrospective explanation does sound a little strained, even if one does not attribute ignorance to his indifference. Yet at the time it was actually *his* works which were regarded as giving adequate musical expression to the Revolution. In July 1917 Asafyev published an article about the composer in the newspaper *New Life* entitled 'The Road to Happiness'. Asafyev regarded the approaching revolution as synonymous with universal happiness and liberation from foreign oppression. And in Prokofiev he saw the musical prophet of these revolutionary aspirations.

I spent the summer of 1917 near Petrograd, completely alone, reading Kant and getting a lot of work done.[129] Of course the significance of Kant for Marxist philosophy would not have dawned on the composer until much later, but at least this reading provided evidence for his biography of serious-minded activity during serious times. News of the October Revolution reached Prokofiev in the spa town of Kislovodsk, where he was visiting his mother. But at that time he was most preoccupied with the idea of going to America. In the summer

Lunacharsky and Mayakovsky in Moscow, 1918

of 1917 he had met the American industrialist Cyrus McCormick, visiting Russia as a member of a diplomatic delegation (the United States had immediately recognized the Provisional Government, but recognition of the Bolshevik State did not follow until 1933). McCormick provided financial support for the printing of the *Scythian Suite* and promised to help the composer should he ever come to America.

Europe was in the midst of war. In the New World Prokofiev might expect a brighter future. It was still possible to get to America via Constantinople. Through Benois and Gorky, with whom Prokofiev had remained in friendly contact even when abroad, the composer had met Lunacharsky. On 21 April 1918 Prokofiev conducted the première of his *Classical Symphony* in Petrograd. The former Court Orchestra was playing and Lunacharsky was in the audience. Prokofiev had the opportunity of putting his proposed trip abroad to him after the concert: *I had been working hard for a long time and now needed a bit of fresh air.* 'Don't you think we now have enough fresh air?' 'Yes, but I mean the physical air of seas and oceans.' Lunacharsky's reply is legendary: 'You are a revolutionary in music and we are so in life – we ought to work together. But if you want to go to America, I will not put anything in your way.'[130] On 17 May 1918 Prokofiev left the Soviet Union. *I had no clear understanding of the vigour or the significance of the October Revolution.*[131]

'Longing for World Culture' [132]

After being detained on the Island for three days and questioned exhaustively ('Have you ever been in jail?' 'Yes.' 'That's bad. Where was that?' 'With you here on this island.' 'Ah, you like to joke!'), I was admitted into the United States. [133] In his autobiography Prokofiev gives a humorous account of the complications of his travels within the United States. Equally memorable are his descriptions of the endless difficulties of his stay: the stiff competition from all over the world and the reserve of American audiences toward contemporary music, the exacting standards of the judgmental music press and the business-like organization and mentality of the concert world, *an entire system of arrangements, deals and contracts.* [134] Once again, however, one should bear in mind the official nature of his retrospective account, written from within the Soviet Union during the 1940s. Prokofiev did not experience the existential distress of many other exiles of this time. Indeed, though used to success, he received more respect and recognition here than many others. Press reports were already heralding him as 'one of the most promising Russian composers after Stravinsky'. [135] And McCormick's extensive connections opened the doors of American musical life to him.

In essential respects the composer's international reputation and the resounding success of many of his works began in America. With his growing popularity, Prokofiev eventually became a well-known personality in public life, over and above his significance purely as an artist. In 1945 *Newsweek* ran a comprehensive biographical article about him, and *Time* Magazine devoted its front page to him as 'Russia's greatest living composer'.[136] Prokofiev's collaboration with America's great orchestras and opera houses, especially in Chicago, Boston, and New York, and with conductors like Koussevitzky, and later Stokowski and Toscanini, ensured the continued currency of his work after his departure and established a Prokofiev tradition in America which remains vigorous today.[137]

Prokofiev's first public appearance in America occurred in the Brooklyn Museum. He performed in a 'Russian Concert' given in conjunction with the opening of an exhibition of work by the St Petersburg artist Boris Anisfeld.[138] The New York critics were initially disappointed, finding in the *Visions fugitives* and *Piano Pieces* Op 12 not the anticipated 'roaring lion' of modernist music but the 'tame lamb'.[139] His real American début however, a solo evening performance in the Aeolian Hall, finally lived up to the expectations of both audience and press. Couched in sensationalist language, the reviews in the New York papers reflect the lively interest of the American musical world in Prokofiev as a representative of the new revolutionary Russia: 'His emotional impassiveness contrasted starkly with the volcanic eruptions from the piano . . . He has fingers of steel, wrists of steel, arms of steel, biceps and triceps of steel, shoulder-blades of steel . . . the finale of the *Second Piano Sonata* evokes the image of a herd of charging mammoths on a high Asiatic plane.'[140] Symphony concerts followed. In Chicago, where Prokofiev played his *First Piano Concerto* and conducted the *Scythian Suite*, this pianist, conductor and composer was hailed as 'a sensational phenomenon'.[141] Certainly the critics could not agree about his music. But Prokofiev himself was 'the musical novelty of the season',[142] an instant celebrity.

After one of his concerts in New York the composer also made the acquaintance of the singer Lina Llubera, his future wife. She came from Madrid, her father's family was Spanish, her mother was from the Alsace, though of Huguenot origin, and growing up in Russian Poland, she had been fluent in Russian from childhood.

Publishers too began to take an interest in his music. The four piano pieces titled *Old Grand-mother's Tales* and the *Four Piano Pieces* Op 32, were both written to commission. They belong to Prokofiev's popular, almost classical works, music at once archaic and playfully refined and full of a characteristic humour, often designated as grotesque. In 1919 Prokofiev met up with a group of émigré Jewish musicians who had studied alongside him in the tolerant atmosphere of the St Petersburg Conservatory under Glazunov; they had formed a

In the United States Prokofiev was hailed as an instant celebrity

chamber group, Zimro, which was dedicated to the performance and creation of specifically Jewish works. Hoping to persuade Prokofiev to write for them, they gave him a notebook filled with a collection of Klezmer themes. Initially he was unwilling to write a work based on folk material. However, they soon won him over and he wrote an *Overture on Hebrew Themes* for piano, clarinet and string quartet, a choice of instrumentation deliberately evoking a traditional Jewish wedding band.

In America Prokofiev was also able to realize some of his plans for opera for the first time. McCormick had introduced him to the Director of the Chicago Opera, Cleofonte Campanini. Among the first things they discussed was a production of his Dostoevsky opera *The Gambler*. Only a piano extract from this work was to hand; the score had been lying in the Mariinsky Theatre in Petrograd since the intended performance there. After a lengthy interruption due to a serious bout of diphtheria and scarlet fever,

Prokofiev wrote another opera, *The Love for Three Oranges*. It was 'the first time that such an assignment had been given to a composer in this country . . . , a commission to produce an opera, not a note of which had been heard by anyone.'[143]

The work is based on Carlo Gozzi's *L'Amore delle Tre Melarance*, the satirical reworking of an ancient fable about melancholy and laughter. It is the story of a prince who cannot laugh and who discovers three princesses inside oranges, the third of whom after many intrigues he marries. Prokofiev came to know the play in the Russian adaptation by Meyerhold, Vladimir Solovyov, and Konstantin Vogar. There is a striking parallel between Meyerhold's development of an anti-realistic concept of theatre in pre-revolutionary Russia, and Gozzi's revival of the theatre of Commedia dell'Arte: both stressed improvisation over character interpretation, imagination over illusionistic imitation, magic over morality, brilliant buffoonery and flights of fancy over outworn stage realism. Here by openly subscribing to the principle of 'as if', the artistic always remains in harmony with the artificial. 'As the game the actors play approaches real life,' according to Meyerhold, the 'dissonance becomes unbearable.'[144]

Meyerhold's 'Entertainment in twelve scenes, Prologue, Epilogue and three Intermezzi', with its episodic structure, presents a complicated story rich in contrasts, interweaving different levels of reality and fantasy, all arranged for stage production. Prokofiev had taken this text with him to America, intending to set it to music. *I was especially delighted by the scenic aspect. Something new was being presented in the three interwoven plots, that of the figures from the fairy-tale (the prince,*

The Love for Three Oranges at ENO
Photograph © Bill Rafferty

Truffaldino etc), that of the infernal powers on whom they are dependent (the magician Celio, the Fata Morgana), and finally that of the freaks representing the Director who comment on events.[145] The freaks personify tragic, comic, lyric, and empty-headed figures, types respectively of all that is serious, entertaining, emotional or dubious – a group of purely conventional operatic characters. They represent the masks of the 'heroes' and are intended to observe the framed action of the play from without. Because of their repeated interference in the action, even this claim to aesthetic distance is shown up to be empty and pretentious.

Prokofiev drew on a variety of traditional elements and forms in his music. *Bearing American tastes in mind, I chose a musical idiom that was simpler than in 'The Gambler'.*[146] The significant moments in the plot are not highlighted by grand arias and ensembles but by dance and pantomime. Through the use of a variety of musical styles, the composer emphasizes the different dramatic strands of the play. With its dry wit, fantastical scurrility and heavily ironic stylization, the music draws attention to the unreality of the events. It is in these devices that the innovative potency of *The Love for Three Oranges* can be seen. The work is not an opera in the traditional sense but represents a significant stage in Prokofiev's search for ways to revitalize this genre. It is also one of the most spirited and amusing stage compositions of the 20th century, sustained by an infectious alternation between jest, satire, irony, and more serious meaning, all of it, as it were, triumphantly proclaiming 'Long live theatre!' (final chorus).

Production of *The Love for Three Oranges* was scheduled for the end of 1919. However Campanini's sudden death disrupted plans for the première; the opera had to be postponed until the following season. Prokofiev, who for nine months had devoted himself solely to this task, feared that he would have to rejoin the concert circuit at once to keep afloat financially. He requested some compensatory remuneration. The request was refused, and, in return, Prokofiev forbade all productions of his opera. The following year, the celebrated singer, Mary Garden (among other things protagonist in the first performance of Debussy's *Pelléas and Mélisande*), took over the directorship of the opera house. She drew up a new contract and at last initiated production of the work. On the first night, Prokofiev himself conducted, but it was Anisfeld's staging that had the most spectacular success. The American public did not show the expected enthusiasm for the music. Only a few performances were given, including a guest performance in New York. Three years later Eugen Szenkar staged the first German production of the opera in Cologne, to much greater acclaim.[147] *It was a very successful production, much truer to the spirit of the original than in America, if also less extravagant. The audience and press too showed greater appreciation than in New York or Chicago.*[148] In 1926 the opera was staged in Leningrad. *I sat next to Lunacharsky during the performance of 'The Love for Three Oranges', and he remarked that the 'Scythian Suite' was something elemental and the 'The Three Oranges' a glass of champagne . . . It was without doubt the best production so far.*[149] Later the opera was only sporadically performed on the Soviet stage.[150] The wit and spirit of Prokofiev's score were not disputed in Russia, but it became a refrain among critics that the work offered no positive alternatives to the empty conventions it held up to ridicule.

Ansermet, Diaghilev, Stravinsky and Prokofiev in London, 1921

As a pianist, however, Prokofiev received unqualified recognition and admiration in America; the monetary success of his concert tours, too enabled him to devote himself increasingly to composition. However, his reputation as a pianist sometimes threatened to eclipse his vocation as a composer; the journal *Musical America* showed photographs of Prokofiev and Stravinsky with the caption: 'The composer Stravinsky and the pianist

Prokofiev.'[151] Prokofiev became impatient. The mere interpretation of other people's work did not satisfy his deeper motivations. He was obsessed with his own music. *Sometimes I would stroll through the huge park in the centre of New York and gazing up at the surrounding skyscrapers think with cold fury about the splendid American orchestras that had no time for my music: about the critics who reiterated 'Beethoven, what a great musical genius' a hundred times and denigrated everything new; about the manager who organized long concert tours with programmes featuring the same old familiar numbers played fifty times already. I had come over far too early: the child, namely America, was not yet old enough for modern music. Home again perhaps? But through which gates? Russia was sealed off on all fronts by the White Guards.*[152]

After the victory of the Bolsheviks at the beginning of 1920, Prokofiev's mother had joined the stream of refugees making their way through Constantinople to Europe. He wanted her to join him in Paris. His mother's flight and other reports from emigrant circles about the political and economic situation in the Soviet Union convinced the composer to postpone his return to Russia until a date in the distant future.

Russian Civil War. In 1918 Anti-Bolshevik groups formed to fight Leon Trotsky's Red Army (from April 1918 Trotsky became the People's Commissionaire for Defence). Dubbed the White Army they varied widely in their political aims and social backgrounds. The war was fought on several fronts. In the Urals and Siberia the White Army was led by Admiral Kolchak. In the south Generals Denikin and Krasnow led campaigns. Other forces were lead by General Judenitsch in Estonia and General Miller in northern Russia. Western allies landed in Vladivostock, Murmansk, Archangel, and the Black Sea ports in order to safeguard their interests.

In February 1919 the Whites rejected an attempt by the American President Woodrow Wilson to mediate between the warring parties, and plans of a 'crusade' by the French Marshal Ferdinand Foch were rejected by the Great Council of the Allies. The lack of any popular support or clear strategy doomed the White Armies to failure. Their offensives were rebuffed by the Red Army's counterattack. In 1920 the last of the White Armies retreated from the Crimean Peninsula.

CIVIL WAR

Prokofiev spent the summer months of 1920 and 1921 in Europe. In London and in Paris he renewed contact with Diaghilev. Prokofiev had always been fascinated by the impresario's busy life, and his fund of new ideas. Diaghilev was still very much interested in the composer, whom he regarded as, after Stravinsky, his 'second son'. On 15 May 1920 the first post-war season of *Les Ballets Russes* opened with a première of Stravisnky's *Pulcinella*. Diaghilev had commissioned Stravinsky to arrange a collection of music purporting to be by the Italian composer Pergolesi. The resulting ballet owes more than a small debt to the transparency and 'spring' of Prokofiev's *Classical Symphony*. The following year the ballet Prokofiev had been commissioned to write five years earlier, *The Buffoon*, was finally to be produced. The composer worked through the score once more, rewriting passages and finishing the orchestration.

The year 1921 brought Prokofiev a number of significant successes. Koussevitzky, just arrived from Russia, and Diaghilev competed enthusiastically for the privilege of the first production of one of his works in Paris. Koussevitzky's performance of the *Scythian Suite* struck the Parisian consciousness like a thunderbolt. Prokofiev had arrived.

The première of the ballet *The Buffoon* at the Théâtre de la Gaité-Lyrique for the opening of Diaghilev's season also created a sensation. It is one of Prokofiev's most eccentric scores. The guileful antics of a fool who makes mock of seven other fools, are followed with much irony and grimacing grotesquerie. The music was perfectly complemented by Mikhail Larionov's costumes and stage décor with their stylized folkish combination of the Russian Lubok's garish colours and their wildly exuberant Cubist forms and figures. A portrait sketch of Prokofiev by Matisse appeared on the programme leaflet. The work remained in the repertoire until the break-up of the *Les Ballets Russes* enterprise itself. At the end of the same year the première of *The Third Piano Concerto* and the opera

The Love for Three Oranges in Chicago provided a further boost to Prokofiev's career as a composer in the West.

During his summer stay in Brittany in 1921, Prokofiev wrote musical settings for five poems by his émigré friend Balmont, who was in the immediate neighbourhood. They are Symbolist nature fantasies, pictures, invocations, and exorcisms. The composer evoked their lurid atmosphere

Larionov's caricature of Prokofiev and members of *Les Ballets Russes* © DACS

through refined harmonic progressions. Prokofiev dedicated these songs, brought together as *Five Songs to Poems by Konstantin Balmont*, Op 36, to Lina Llubera.

In the *Third Piano Concerto* Prokofiev was able to return to a longer, more speculative project. He had already made notes for some of its themes in Russia, which included an idea for an unfinished string quartet *on the white notes.* (Perhaps this was the germ of the *Second Quartet*) The *Concerto* is dedicated to Balmont. Prokofiev played bits of the music out to him, inspiring the poet to write his poem *Third Concerto*:

A joyous blaze of purple flowers,
The instrument of words plays little flames,
Which suddenly stick out little tongues of fire.
From molten ore a stream has risen.
Moments dance to waltzes, centuries lead gavottes.
Suddenly a primeval beast, startled by enemies,
Bursts from its trammels, charges with lowered horns.
Yet hark, a gentle sound in the distance.
Children are building castles with shells;
How pretty the ramparts built with opal.
But the wild foaming tide throws all in a heap.

But wild foams the tide, covering all:
Prokofiev! Music and youth now flourish,
In you the orchestra yearned for sonorous flights
And the invincible Scythian beats the sun's tambourine.[153]

The *Third Concerto* was premièred on 16 December 1921, conducted by Frederick Stock. The composer played the virtuoso piano part, with the Chicago Symphony Orchestra accompanying. There is a certain underlying tone of placid optimism about this concerto, which has made it one of Prokofiev's most popular works. It was the performance of this work on numerous concert tours in subsequent years that helped consolidate his reputation as a composer retroactively throughout the Western world. And it was also with the *Third Piano Concerto* that Prokofiev scored further triumphs on his first trip to the Soviet Union in 1927. The element of extreme virtuosity and the lively combination of acuteness and precision, energy and discipline with elements of lyricism and passion, of radiance and capriciousness are among the features that account for the special place the work has achieved in music beyond the Prokofiev canon.

In 1922 Prokofiev again took up residence in Europe on a permanent basis, first in Kloster Ettal, a Benedictine abbey in Bavaria, then at the end of 1923 in Paris. After 1936 he returned to the Soviet Union, but continued to keep in touch with his personal contacts. Regular concert tours during the winter months still took him back to America frequently.

In March 1922 I moved to southern Germany near Kloster Ettal in the foothills of the Bavarian Alps, three kilometres from Oberammergau . . . , a picturesque and tranquil region, absolutely ideal for working.[154]

Prokofiev's stay in this idyllic place, initially planned for a year, lasted for nearly two years. Here he lived with his mother and his friend Boris Bashkirov (who worked, as a poet under the name of Boris Werin), and received visits, with increasing frequency, from Lina Llubera, who was completing her singing studies in Paris. They went on long walks together in the surrounding countryside, and sometimes further afield. 'Sergey Sergeyevich used to carry a thick book on botany with him, a subject which at the time, and indeed even in childhood, had interested him deeply. We would collect flowers and plants during our walks, looking up their names and sorting them into categories, so we frequently had to consult this book. Whenever he found a wildflower he had known in childhood, he would be absolutely delighted, as though he had met an old friend. It would remind him of Sontsovka and its fields.'[155] In September 1923 Lina Llubera, pregnant with their first son, and Sergey Prokofiev were married in a civil ceremony in Kloster Ettal.

From Bavaria Prokofiev made a number of trips to keep in touch with Europe's concert world. In Paris he played his *Third Piano Concerto* several times under Koussevitzky's baton. He also resumed his association with Koussevitzky's Gutheil Press, which had been reestablished in Paris, and was now able to publish numerous compositions he had written over the previous ten years. Back in Ettal he prepared the piano excerpts from his *The Love for Three Oranges* and *The Buffoon* for printing, and assembled a symphonic suite based on the ballet. He composed the *Fifth Piano Sonata* here and revised his *Second Piano Concerto*. But above all he devoted himself – inspired by the *wonderful quiet where one can sit still and create great works,*[156] and also, on his own admission by the mystical spirit of the monastic surroundings – to further work on his new opera, *The Fiery Angel*.

The theme of Valeri Bryusov's great Symbolist novella, on which the opera was based, is the contradictory roles of science and humanism and of religion and occultism in Europe during the Inquisition. The author described what he was trying to convey in a foreword: 'In the 16th century the dubious magical practices and soothsayings of the Middle Ages came to be regarded as branches of exact science . . . The spirit of the century, which was at pains to subordinate everything to reason, managed to transform magic too into a rational doctrine, made soothsaying a matter of reason and logic, and placed the flight to the Witches' Sabbath on a scientific footing.'[157] The contrast between this image-laden story about the erotically and spiritually anguished Renate, the returnee from America, Sir Rupert, the 'fiery angel' Madiel and his worldly incarnation, Henry, and Prokofiev's recently completed Gozzi opera could not have been starker.

After the gay light-hearted oranges it was challenging to take on the passion-embroiled figure of Renate. The medieval background[158] *with its travelling Faust figures and cursing archbishops was also tempting.*[159]

Again the composer again wrote the libretto himself. The complicated plot could hardly be managed effectively for the stage except, much as later in *War and Peace*, through a series of separate self-contained episodes. Prokofiev organized the text (which Bryusov had presented as Rupert's narrative) into seven scenes: Rupert's meeting with Renate in the hostel room / Search for Henry in Cologne with the help of John Glock's magic books and the knowledge of the thrice-Doctor Agrippa of Nettesheim / Meeting with Henry outside his house / Duel between Rupert and Henry on the banks of the Rhein, in which the former has been forbidden by Renate to do Henry any harm and is thus himself severely wounded / Renate's parting from Rupert after his convalescence (Doctor: '*My friend, we do not live in Hunnish times. In the 16th century nothing is impossible for medicine.*'[160]) Rupert's joining up with Mephistopheles and Faust / Inquisition, exorcisms, commotion, and ecstasy among the nuns in the abbey undercroft over Renate's sentencing (the Inquisitor *screams with rage while piercing Renate with his staff: 'This woman is guilty of having had carnal relations with Satan. May she be delivered to the Inquisition's court of punishment. To the rack with the witch, let her burn.*'[161]) The original ending with the (natural) death of Renate was eliminated. *On the stage it didn't make an impact, and in the presence of Faust and Mephisto was also a little too reminiscent of Gretchen's death. And as despite all manner of contrivances I had not managed to avoid a rather static effect in the previous acts, I got rid of the last scene (musically it did not*

contain anything much new in any case), and decided to end things with
ecstatic cries. Should the audience happen to have nodded off in the course
of the opera, at least they would wake up again before the final curtain.[162]

Prokofiev had turned to similar subject matter once before in his
youthful opera *Maddalena*, which also deals with a protagonist torn
by inner conflict. Now, at the height of his powers as a composer,
working through the intricacies scene by scene, he succeeded in
creating a masterly musical rendition of the apocalyptic tensions
contained in the material. Prokofiev achieved something quite
extraordinary here. *The Fiery Angel* is musically his most impressive
stage work, one of the major operas of the 20th century. Within the
formal closed-circuitry of the sequence of scenes, a complex web of
leitmotifs and themes is suggested. The themes,[163] some of which
hark back to earlier works, are discernible not only in the vividly
conceived protagonists but also in the localities, the abstract concepts (opposition between heavenly and Satanic messengers), the
magic rituals (struggle for Renate's soul), and the romantic episodes
(the tenderness of true love). At the climactic points in the opera
the groundswell of the declamatory recitative intensifies to an
aria-like pitch of dramatic expressiveness, somewhere between
transcendent ecstasy and shuddering terror. Here the demands
made by the composer on the singers' voices, especially that of
Renate, border on the limits of physical possibility. There is a
correlation between the instrumental employment of the vocal
element and the interweaving of the orchestral phrases with the
dramatic action. On the one hand the dense leitmotif-laden orchestral polyphony supports the development of the plot, on the other,
symphonic interludes communicate a sense of its dramatic unity.

A production of the opera seemed impossible at first, and
Prokofiev would have trouble with this work for a decade to come.
Negotiations with theatres in Europe and America made never-
ending reworkings necessary. The composer was especially disillu-
sioned when Bruno Walter backed out of the production planned

for the autumn of 1927 in Berlin. Or at least he was not prepared to accept his own late submission of the orchestral material as an adequate excuse: *In my opinion Bruno Walter acted dishonourably. If he could not manage it in time for the autumn, he could have brought out the opera in the spring.*[164] Koussevitzky, once again, introduced the public to excerpts from the second act in a concert in Paris. Prokofiev himself tried to salvage the score by reworking it for his *Third Symphony, one of my most significant compositions.*[165] Technical difficulties, above all stood in the way of staging the opera: the long and prominent part of Renate, the difficult handling of the chorus, the enormous demands on the orchestra. It was only after the composer's death that the opera had its first performance: in concert at the Paris Opera theatre in 1954, and on stage in Venice in September 1955.

Even during his sojourn in Kloster Ettal, Paris remained the centre of his musical world. He kept abreast of developments there, whilst remaining oddly uninterested in the musical revolution that was shaking Vienna.

The French capital was also to become for ten years the centre of his personal world. Here the composer's mother died at the end of 1924, and his two sons, Sviatoslav and Oleg, were born in 1924 and 1928. And it was here too that his involvement with the religious community of Christian Scientists developed.

In the 1920s Paris was regarded at the capital of the artistic world. The first decade after the war had seen the experimentation of the avant-garde, 'actions' and manifestos, often in that narrow border region between artistic statement and social provocation. By the time that Erik Satie, elevated by Jean Cocteau to the status of musical pontif of this movement, died in 1925, traditional aesthetic criteria were again being increasingly expected of music. Yet the French composers, represented by the '*Les Six*', stood as firmly opposed to Romanticism and Impressionism, to the spirits of Wagner and Debussy, as to the various Expressionisms of Skryabin or Schoenberg. Their return to a functional emphasis in art demanded more direct, open musical idioms, involving concise forms and clear sounds.

Paris was the meeting place for artists from the Old World and the New. Gertrude Stein gathered the 'lost generation' of American writers round her, Ernest Hemingway, John Dos Passos and e e cummings. Here painters such as Chagall and Max Ernst became 'French' artists. And the most 'Parisian' of musicians included Koussevitzky, Diaghilev, and Stravinsky.

Prokofiev performed a whole series of his works in Paris, though almost exclusively the products of his Russian period. On 18 October 1923 Koussevitzky conducted the delayed première of the *First Violin Concerto* with the leader of his orchestra Marcel Darrieux. The première had originally been scheduled to take place in Moscow

Les Six. In 1917 six composers assembled under the leadership of Jean Cocteau, and influenced by Erik Satie. The composers were Germaine Tailleferre, Francois Poulenc, Honegger, Durey, Auric and Darius Milhaud. Their bond was primarily one of friendship, rather than a particularly strict artistic agenda. The group declared that they would draw their influence from everyday life, incorporating the sounds of modern life, be they machines, the music hall, the circus and the jazz that was sweeping Paris. Not much else unified them, save a shared admiration for the vanguard of the European avant-garde, particularly Schoenberg and Bartok, whose music featured in their innovative programmes. In 1923, Prokofiev wrote to Poulenc from Kloster Ettal that a Moscow music journal was interested in his music, and that of Darius Milhaud, and that he wished to help publicize *Les Six's* work in Moscow. Poulenc wrote back immediately expressing his admiration for Prokofiev's beautifully constructed music and playing: *'J'aime infinement votre musique . . .'.*

in October 1917, but this concert was overtaken by the events of that month and had proved impossible to reorganize. (The original violinist, Paul Kochanski later premièred the *Cinq Melodies* Op 35.) The audience included a cross section of Parisian artistic elite including Picasso, Pavlova, Arthur Rubinstein, and Joseph Szigeti, who later revised and popularized the concerto.[166] *The critics were divided, seemingly irked that the new work was too conventional.*[167] The *Fifth Piano Sonata* too was *only hesitantly accepted.*[168] Even the revised

Second Piano Concerto did not receive any special attention, not at all like the sensation it had caused at its first performance in Pavlovsk. Only the cantata *Seven, They are Seven* was an outstanding success:[169] 'It is grandiose and awesome and primitive, without doubt the most effective of Prokofiev's compositions.'[170] It seemed as difficult to entertain Parisian audiences as to shock them. *Moving to Paris does not mean becoming a Parisian.*[171] *. . . Here for the first time a complaint was made which I would often hear again – that I warmed up old material. I resolved to compose a large-scale symphony.*[172] Prokofiev hoped that with this work he would finally establish himself in Europe as a European composer.

A large-scale scale symphony! In France! In 1924! With a work like this Prokofiev was placing himself outside all the compositional developments current in Western Europe at the time. The history of the symphony, as a genre with special claims and a specific content, seemed to have come to an end. Excepting perhaps its continuing validity in Britain, Scandinavia, and Russia. It was only in the 1930s that it again became an intense focus of interest for composers. Prokofiev had not been trying to continue this tradition when he wrote his *Classical Symphony* (which he now also designated his *First Symphony*), but with his *Second Symphony* the composer finally made formal acknowledgement to Beethoven. The latter's last piano sonata Op 111 served as the model for a two-part cyclic composition, which Prokofiev rounded out by recapitulating the thematic material from the introductory 'Allegro ben articolato' in the last of the six variations of the second movement. For the emotional content of the genre, on the other hand he had recourse to trends in the musical idiom of the avant-garde. Not unlike his collaborator's in 'Triton' Milhaud in his *Agricultural Machines* (1919), Honegger in *Pacific 231* (1923) and the 'Pianist Futurist' George Antheil in his piano sonatas, Prokofiev paid homage to the myth of the machine, the mechanisms of the technological age. It was to be a *Symphony of Iron and Steel*,[173] stark and shocking and, above all, modern. Prokofiev's

Second Symphony is an expansive work, composed for comprehensive orchestral equipment, conceptually complex, and lavishly scored for a huge orchestra. In the finale its chromaticism collapses into 'twelve-tone' chords. Its aggressiveness of sound has striking affinities with works such as the *Scythian Suite* or the cantata *Seven, They are Seven*. But the many effects are intensified still further by the fierce agitation of crass dynamic tensions and the ever-increasing pitch, from the leaping tenths in the main theme of the first movement onwards.

The symphony represents the furthest step in the development of richly dissonant language in all of Prokofiev's oeuvre. Its acceptance proved correspondingly difficult. The composer described the work as *a complicated thing*,[174] unwieldy and difficult, and was plagued by doubts about the success of his work. *The symphony aroused nothing but bewilderment . . . Could it really be possible that, despite my long years of experience and my high level of technical proficiency, I had got completely bogged down, and this after nine months of the most strenuous application?*[175] At all events, Prokofiev's hopes of finally being recognized were not fulfilled with his work.

George Antheil (1900–59) was the most notorious American composer and performer of the inter-war years. After studying privately with Ernest Bloch, he went to Europe in 1922, where he toured as a virtuoso pianist, playing his violent and mechanistic piano works. He was noted for his methods: once he quieted a restive German audience by ordering the doors of the concert hall to be locked, taking a revolver from the silk shoulder holster which he always wore and placing it on the piano, then resumed playing. In Paris, he moved in the circles of Stein, Joyce, and Pound, and collaborated with Leger on *Ballet Mecanique*, which to his intense pleasure degenerated into the biggest concert hall fist-fight since the première of *Le Sacre du Printemps* fourteen years earlier. He perhaps overestimated the importance of the machine, and, rather late, sought to put Marinetti's doctrines into musical form. Later in life he ran an agony column and collaborated with Hedy Lamarr on the development of a patented naval communication device for controlling torpedoes. He had some impact on Prokofiev; the sound world of his *Seventh Sonata* is directly derived from Antheil's thunderous pianism, which he had heard two decades earlier. He married Arthur Schnitzler's niece.

A COMPLICATED THING

It was perhaps the only occasion when I was visited by the fear of being doomed to play the part of a second rate composer.[176]

Besides this large symphony, *in order to earn some money*[177] Prokofiev composed a short ballet, *Trapeze*, for a travelling troupe run by the Russian ballet master Boris Romanov. The subject matter was drawn from circus life. The music is abstract, and makes no attempt at concrete illustration of the events on stage. Prokofiev arranged it into a six movement quintet, (scored for oboe, clarinet, violin, viola, and double-bass), so as to make it available as pure chamber music (*Quintet* Op 39) and maximize sales. Despite its formal 'divertimento' character, the work is not by any means easy to play or dance. It is harmonically dense and dissonant, containing *several rhythmic difficulties such as tunes in ten-eight time (3-4-3); the ballet master was left to carry the can for all of this.*[178] The *Quintet* has gained a deserved reputation as one of the most demanding and virtuoso chamber works of the 20th century.

In the summer of 1925 the composer received a new commission from Diaghilev, *Le Pas D'Acier*. The following winter, for the first time in four years, Prokofiev was back in the United States. He gave evening solo piano recitals, song recitals with his wife Lina Llubera, and numerous symphony concerts with the Boston Symphony Orchestra, which for two years had been under Koussevitzky's direction.

In America Prokofiev had the opportunity to make recordings of a number of his piano pieces. The tour was a great success, reconfirming Prokofiev's reputation in America. The composer and his wife became popular society guests. *In one provincial town the club members (300 of them) wanted to shake hands with us after the concert. This ceremony proceeded as follows: each club member stepped up to the Secretary and said: 'I am Mr Smith.' The Chairman then said to me: 'Allow me to introduce you to Mr Smith!' I shook hands with him and said 'Delighted, Mr Smith!' Mr Smith said 'Delighted, Mr Prokofiev' and went on to my wife. Meanwhile Mr Jones approached in the same manner, and so forth three hundred times.*[179] Concerts in Italy followed. In Rome Prokofiev had an audience with Pope Pius XI, and in Naples he visited the writer Maxim Gorky. On his return the composer began preparing, in consultation with Meyerhold, for his first trip back to the Soviet Union. From 1927 on he made regular visits, and was continually on the lookout for ways to return to Russia permanently, even though this was repeatedly postponed.

Meanwhile Prokofiev could hardly complain of a lack of acclaim. In Berlin, a ballet titled *The Redeemed* based on the music of the *Scythian Suite* was premièred, and in Buenos Aires this music also appeared in a stage adaptation. With the Moscow première of *The Love for Three Oranges*, a work by the composer appeared on the stage of the Bolshoi Theatre for the first time. In Paris the first performance of *Le Pas D'Acier* became a major event, whilst in London the production of the same ballet was the sensation of the season. On the opening night of a series of Koussevitzky concerts, another piece by Prokofiev was also on the programme, the suite from *The Love for Three Oranges*. A little later Koussevitzky conducted a concert version of the new ballet in Boston. In Kiev *The Buffoon* was put on. The *Second Symphony*, despite its lack of popular appeal, was also performed several more times in Paris. Moscow resounded with the first performance of the suite from the ballet *Le Pas D'Acier*. Koussevitzky conducted excerpts

Sergey Koussevitzky (1874–1951) was, in his time, probably the most important Russian conductor. He was born in Vismy-Volochokr, near Moscow, and first came to attention playing double-bass in the Moscow Philharmonic Society. He founded *Editions Russes de Musique*, which published many works by Stravinsky, Skryabin, and Prokofiev. Together with Belayev, he was Skryabin's first great advocate and benefactor. He stayed in Russia until 1920, when he conducted a successful series of concerts in Paris. Despite his lack of basic score-reading abilities, he succeeded Pierre Monteux as conductor of the Boston Symphony Orchestra. There he conducted an extraordinary series of premières, including Bartok's most popular orchestral work, the *Concerto for Orchestra*, and championed the music of American composers, the first major European conductor to do so.

for the ballet *The Fiery Angel* in concert, with Nina Koshets as Renate. Diaghilev opened the 1929 season in Monte Carlo, shortly before his death, with a production of a new ballet by Prokofiev, *The Prodigal Son*,[180] choreographed by George Balanchine. For the first time there were now two works by the composer, besides *Le Pas D'Acier*, in the repertoire of the *Ballets Russes* at the same time. During the same season the first performance of Prokofiev's *Third Symphony*, conducted by Pierre Monteux, and the Paris première of his ballet *The Prodigal Son* also took place. And of great importance to the composer, his opera *The Gambler* was successfully staged at the Royal Theatre in Brussels, and this ran for three seasons.

Prokofiev's works secured him considerable financial independence. He spent the summer months far from Paris in rented villas and castles: in St Palais-sur-mer outside Royan, at Château de Vetraz near the Swiss border, at Château de la Flechère in Culoz in central France. He continued to compose new works: an *American Overture*, a *Divertimento*, the *Third Symphony*, the piano pieces *Things in Themselves*, and the ballet *The Prodigal Son*. From now, until the composer moved back to the Soviet Union, Mikhail Astrov, an assistant in Koussevitzky's publishing house, acted as his personal

secretary and copyist. A nanny helped Lina with their two sons, and they had a cook and other servants to run the household. Prokofiev bought his first motorcar, a toy for his leisure hours.

In October 1929, after six years without any fixed address in France, the Prokofievs took a permanent apartment in Paris. That autumn he returned to play in Moscow, before undertaking an extended winter tour through the United States, Canada, and Cuba. For Prokofiev the 1920s

Prokofiev and Asafyev on Lake Geneva

were characterized by incessant changes of location, until his final move to the Soviet Union, and even beyond that until his last tour through Western Europe and the United States.

The works of this period reveal a continuing search for new modes of expression. *The Prodigal Son* already begins to show the lyrical seriousness and sober plasticity of many of Prokofiev's Soviet works. In line with his tendency to re-use successful material, Prokofiev reworked this ballet twice. This produced the *Fourth Symphony*, a commission to commemorate the Boston Symphony Orchestra's 50th anniversary, and a *Symphonic Suite* Op 46a. Neither composition found much favour. In 1947, after completing his *Fifth* and *Sixth Symphonies*, Prokofiev rewrote the *Fourth Symphony* as Op 112. A commission from America also produced the *'First String Quartet'*, which the library of Congress in Washington wanted from me. This huge library is inferior to the European ones in as much as its manuscript department does not have extensive holdings. To improve them a fund was set up with which chamber music was commissioned from contemporary composers, as a way of receiving further manuscripts.[181]

For the first time in five years he again began to write piano music: *Things in Themselves*, two *Sonatinas* in E minor and G major, *Three Pieces for Piano* Op 59 and three piano pieces titled *Meditations*. These works reflect a retrospective attitude, lyrically restrained rather than forward-driving. It is music for a small circle of connoisseurs, at once exclusive and intimate.

In 1931 Prokofiev wrote his *Fourth Piano Concerto* (for the left hand only), commissioned by the Austrian pianist Paul Wittgenstein.[182] *He had lost his right hand at the front and put all his energies into developing the left one, as well as all his money into acquiring a suitable concert repertoire. But he did not have much luck with it, and Richard Strauss composed symphonic studies with an orchestra four times too loud for him. 'How am I to tackle such an orchestra with one miserable hand!' cried Wittgenstein in utter despair . . . Ravel wrote a concerto for him which begins with a huge cadenza for the left hand. 'If I wanted to play without an*

'Triton'. On 13 March 1932, Prokofiev wrote to his friend Vladimir Dukelsky, later famous as the light music composer Vernon Duke. 'Please find out from Kochanski what has prevented him from sending me the score of my sonata for two violins.' He wrote to Myaskovsky on 27 July from Paris; 'You cannot imagine what sort of crisis there is here among all the music publishers, I have become a member of the permanent jury of a new chamber music society in Paris, 'Triton', which will inaugurate its activity beginning in the autumn.'

'Triton' gave twice-monthly concerts of new chamber music played and sung by a variety of musicians, taking advantage of the extraordinary cross-section of international virtuosi and composers who had taken up residence in Paris, it was founded by Pierre Octave-Ferroud, alongside

Florent Schmitt and Poulenc.

On 16 December 1932, the ballet *On the Banks of the Dnieper*, which was translated as *Ballet sur le Borysthène*, premièred in Paris. On the same night, Prokofiev's *Sonata for Two Violins* received its French première, at the launch of 'Triton' at the École Normale de Musique. This concert had been organized by Prokofiev in collaboration with, amongst others, Honneger, Milhaud and Poulenc. He wrote, *'Fortunately, the ballet came half an hour later, and so, immediately after the Sonata we dashed over to the opera; musicians, critics, composer, all together.'* The rest of the programme comprised chamber works by the Swiss composer Honneger, Lázló Lajtha, Roussel, and Fauré. The opera was an unqualified flop. In 1933 Myaskovsky wrote: 'Prokofiev sent me his *Sonata for Two Violins*, it is rather strange . . .'.

orchestra, I would not have ordered a concerto for orchestra!' said Wittgenstein angrily . . .[183] Prokofiev foresaw problems with this work, even while composing, because of Wittgenstein's musical ideals: *I hoped this concerto would meet with your approval both as a pianist and with regard to the balance between piano and orchestra. But I've been racking my brains trying to imagine what impression it will make on you as music. A difficult problem! You are a musician of the 19th century, I of the 20th century.*[184] The composer's imagination had not deceived him: *When I sent Wittgenstein my concerto he wrote back: 'Thank you for your concerto, but I don't understand a note of it and will never play it!'*[185]

Critics in both the East and West pronounced a remarkably unanimous verdict on Prokofiev's *Fifth Piano Concerto*, which the composer first performed in 1932 in a concert with the Berlin

Philharmonic under Wilhelm Furt-wängler. This five-part work is as much characterized by strict rational calculation as it is by playful experimentation. The foreground is dominated for long stretches by the driving toccata-like aspect of Prokofiev's piano style, vehement, vital, and virtuoso. In between, lyrical episodes appear. 'A mish-mash of empty sound-play, impressionism, a banal stridency which sometimes gives the piano the feel of a percussion instrument, Asiatic wildness and classicising occludedness,' concluded the *Zeitschrift für Musik*, 'the whole thing is more a matter of acrobatics than of art.'[186] A similar background chorus of opprobrium that led a tribunal set up by the Central Committee of the Soviet Communist Party in 1948 to disqualify this concerto from performance.

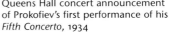

Queens Hall concert announcement of Prokofiev's first performance of his *Fifth Concerto*, 1934

Prokofiev himself later came to associate the work with the difficulties of his quest for a 'new lucidity': *I was looking for simplicity, but feared nothing so much as lapsing into repetition of old turns of phrase with such simplicity, into an 'old simplicity' which is ill suited to today's composers. In my quest I was unwaveringly after a 'new simplicity' and then it transpired that when this was achieved in a new way and above all with a new intonation it was simply not recognized as such . . . ; but I did not lose hope that a whole series . . . of passages might nevertheless with time prove to be indeed simple, once the ear has become accustomed to the new intonations, that is, once these intonations have been naturalized.*[187]

Slow Return Home

Prokofiev's departure from his Russian homeland in 1918, when it was in a state of revolutionary turmoil and civil war, was bound to meet with the criticism and incomprehension of his Soviet biographers.[188] The composer himself later endorsed this verdict through appropriate expressions of remorse: *That was how I let slip the chance of taking an active part in the building of Soviet life . . . In vain did a clever man say to me: 'You are running away from events which will not forgive you for it. When you return you will not be understood.' I did not listen to him.*[189] It is certain, however, that the fledgling Soviet Union would not have provided the basis for a secure artistic career. Artists, especially musicians, whose social relevance is hard enough to determine, found it next to impossible to evade oppressive professional and living conditions, even if they subscribed to the new political order. Prokofiev had spent much time in the West, in the preceding years in Paris, in London, and in Italy. A concert tour to the United States was already planned.

Prokofiev liked to present himself as an apolitical musician: *For my part, I don't bother with politics; Art has nothing to do with it.*[190] His stay abroad, as he himself repeatedly affirmed, had been a matter of personal artistic development, not a permanent exile, and he had left the Soviet Union with the express support of Lunacharsky. *I received an overseas passport and accompanying testimonial that I was embarking on the journey in connection with art and for the restoration of my health. No expiry date was given in the document.*[191] Immediately upon his arrival in the United States he wrote to Diaghilev: *I intend to stay several months here before going back to Russia.*[192]

Personal circumstances had initially delayed Prokofiev's return; his marriage in 1923, the birth of his son, his mother's flight in the aftermath of the 'counterrevolution', and her death in 1924. During these years the composer turned down concert offers from Leningrad. But from the very beginning of his sojourn in the West he sought every opportunity to obtain current information, about not only artistic, but also political developments in the Soviet Union.

Under the pressure of economic decline, the utopian euphoria of 'War Communism' was soon bound to give way to the propaganda-driven normality of the 'New Economic Policy' (NEP). Of course, the political upheavals had not left the structure of musical life untouched. State ownership, by decree, included the theatres, concert organizations and conservatories, the publishing houses, libraries, and archives. The opera houses and concert halls opened their doors to new audiences: workers, peasants and soldiers. Musical education was open to everyone, and free of charge. Yet the reciprocal interaction that Lenin had visualized between art and politics, so widely aspired to, in practice hardly took effect during the early years of the Soviet Union. More remarkably, pre-revolutionary artistic movements continued to flourish after the political watershed.

It was not the October Revolution, but the Stalinism of the 1930s that marked a terrifying turning point, one that became highly relevant to the whole history of music.

The 'Futurist experiment' was actually given new legitimacy by the revolutionary events. But by the same token the proletarian movement, with its provocative hostility to art, also appealed to the anti-bourgeois impulses behind the Revolution. While preservation of the classical heritage had to contend with Lenin's naively romantic taste in art, Anatoly Lunacharsky, the cultivated, resourceful and undogmatic People's Commissar for Education, himself active as a writer, scholar and journalist,[193] succeeded not only in neutralizing polar extremism but in coordinating Russia's unprecedented cultural pluralism. Thanks to his personal integrity, he was also able to win over many of the most significant artists, even when they did not unreservedly sympathize with the political system, to take organizational roles within the new state; Chagall, Kandinsky, Meyerhold, Ehrenburg, and Alexander Blok to name a few. Arthur Lourié was placed in charge of questions of music, himself a visionary modernist, and unflinching promoter of all things new in music.[194]

Under Lunacharsky's cultural commissariat, the opera and theatre companies continued to offer their traditional programme: Tchaikovsky, Rossini, Verdi and Wagner. The Russian Association of Proletarian Musicians (RAPM) was looking for a musical language of programmatic simplicity in service of the masses. Meanwhile, the Association for Contemporary Music (ASM) pursued its avant-garde experiments, exemplified by the idiosyncratic tonal systems of composers such as Nikolay Roslavetz, Nikolay Obuchov, Lourié, Yefim Golycheff, Ivan Vyshnegradski, and Joseph Schillinger. From its centres in Leningrad and Moscow it developed an impressive programme of exchange with contemporary Western music, in coordination with the International Society for Contemporary Music (ISCM).[195] The man who specifically fostered cultural contact with defeated Germany was Georgi Tchitcherin, one of Lenin's companions in exile and Trotsky's successor as People's Commissar for Foreign Affairs and, like Lunacharsky, a cultivated, worldly person interested in music.[196] The Soviet state publishers and the Viennese Universal Edition organized the exchange of scores, and international conductors and soloists took advantage of the opportunities for guest performances.

At the centre of things of course were performances of modernist Western music. Schoenberg, Milhaud, Hindemith and Honegger conducted their own music in the Soviet Union. Only weeks after its first performance in Berlin, Alban Berg travelled to the Leningrad première of his *Wozzeck*. Instrumental works by Stravinsky, Bartok, and Ravel appeared on concert programmes. Operas by Strauss, Schreker, and Křenek were staged in various venues and even in the provinces.[197] Conversely, works by Soviet composers were increasingly performed in the West, often courtesy of Prokofiev's mediation. On the programmes of festivals sponsored by the International Society for Contemporary Music compositions by Mossolov, the constructivist composer *par excellence*, Myaskovsky, Protopopov, Roslavetz, Shenschin, and Tcherepnin appeared. Bruno Walter's performance of Shostakovich's *First Symphony* in Berlin laid the foundation for the latter's international breakthrough.

It was against this background of widespread artistic pluralism and open cultural exchange with the West that the process of Sergey Prokofiev's reintegration into Soviet musical life was played out. The laconic pragmatism of his music, 'his rough-hewn sarcasm, his jests, his hearty laughter, the wild open robust structures'[198] were regarded as the quintessential expression of post-Futurist music in the late 1920s. Prokofiev was much played, discussed and imitated by young composers, and his works were once more regularly featured in the Leningrad Evenings for Contemporary Music. Compositions such as the *Third Piano Concerto* and the *Scythian Suite* were played repeatedly in Moscow. In 1923 three of his *Romances* Op 36 were premièred there, and Pierre Monteux conducted the first production of the ballet *The Buffoon* during a guest visit in 1926. The same year a production of *The Love for Three Oranges* was staged in Leningrad. It ran for a total of forty-nine performances. The possibility of putting on the Dostoevsky opera *The Gambler* continued to be discussed. As early as 1922, under still extraordinarily difficult economic conditions, the music editor of the State Publishing Company had begun to publish Prokofiev's works. An exhibition in Moscow showcased his latest compositions. Prokofiev's music was, as Myaskovsky wrote to him, 'unrivalled in popularity'.[199]

The Soviet press followed Prokofiev's activities indefatigably. The journal of the Association for Contemporary Music, *Towards New Shores* devoted a large part of its first number in April 1923 to the composer, with contributions by Asafyev (under the pseudonym of Igor Glebov) and Samuel Feinberg. Following a request by this journal, Prokofiev himself gave a summary of his *Years of Homelessness* in several lengthy letters;[200] in its New Year's issue of 1925, the Leningrad journal *Life of Art* paid tribute to Prokofiev as one of the great Russian musicians, one who had lived abroad for years and whose return had been eagerly awaited.

From the beginning, the West had regarded Prokofiev as a representative of Soviet culture. Especially in the United States, his 'revolutionary' works inevitably acquired a political dimension: 'He is truly a revolutionary artist. The workers should listen to his music, which is animated by the spirit of freedom.'[201] People talked about his 'Bolshevistic harmonies'.[202] The composer's participation in the concerts of a group of 'Friends of Soviet Russia' could only add to this reputation. In interview statements too, though diffident initially, Prokofiev soon left little doubt about his deep allegiance to his country. In 1921 he declared to the *Pacific Coast Musician*, *The Bolsheviks promote the arts and do their best to encourage their development . . . I am convinced that music in Russia has a great future.*[203]

During his stay in Kloster Ettal he found the time to renew his intimacy with friends who had remained behind in the Soviet Union – Myaskovsky, Derzhanovsky and Asafyev. He also came to grips with more recent Soviet literature. He was in touch with Meyerhold and Mayakovsky, as well as the playwright Alexander Afinogenov and the film director Sergey Eisenstein.

His repeated return visits from 1927 onwards had the greatest importance for the composer's bid to return to his native land after ten years' absence: *I am returning home so that my long absence does not totally estrange me from my countrymen.*[204]

Prokofiev recorded his first journey to the Soviet Union in 1927 in a detailed diary. This was recently made available by the estate of the composer's sons after the death of his wife Lina. If in his autobiography written in the 1940s Prokofiev emphasized his *excitement* and *enthusiasm*[205] on crossing the Soviet border, what emerges from the diary are above all feelings of fear and misgiving: *Over and over it crossed our minds: 'this is our last chance to turn back, it is still not too late. Ah well, even if we perhaps regret it later, and even if it turns out to be a matter of life and death, it has to be!' . . . Our heads filled with such thoughts, as we got into the train and travelled toward the intimidating and fear-inspiring USSR.*[206]

At the height of his international reputation, Prokofiev's journey, became a triumphal procession. He was received with almost limitless sympathy and understanding and with spontaneous enthusiasm in overcrowded concert halls. *I don't think I have ever had such a reception anywhere.*[207] The composer gave concerts for ten weeks, in Moscow hosted by 'Persifams', the orchestra without a conductor,

in Leningrad, in Kharkov, Kiev and Odessa, everywhere performing his own works. Numerous extra concerts had to be arranged. Everywhere he met old friends and colleagues, Myaskovsky, Asafyev, Derzhanovsky, Vera Alpers, and his teacher Glazunov.[208]

All the young Leningrad composers had assembled in my honour . . . There was a long list of works I was supposed to listen to, and so we set to work at once.

The first was Schillinger, who played a complicated and uninteresting piece . . .

The next to play was Shostakovich, a very young man who is not only a composer but a pianist. He gave me the score and bravely played by heart. His sonata opens with a lively double

'Persifams' was an attempt to put revolutionary theory to work in orchestral practice. It was founded in 1922 and survived until 1932, when it was suppressed, charged with being an example of 'bourgeois democracy'. The membership of this virtuoso symphony orchestra, which sat in a circle, and played without a conductor, was drawn from the best players from the Bolshoi Orchestra and the Moscow Conservatory. Its subscription concerts in the Great Hall of the Moscow Conservatory were extremely influential, and the organization spawned a tradition of virtuoso autonomous orchestras in the Eastern bloc. Prokofiev and Milhaud were among the many composers who were inspired to write new works by this ensemble's sensitive virtuosity .

79

counterpoint in the style of Bach. In the second movement which follows without a pause, soft harmonies predominate, and there is also a melody in the middle – very beautiful, if a little long drawn out, perhaps too long. This andante modulates into a brisk finale, which in comparison to the other movements is disproportionately short. At all events, after Schillinger it was so much more lively and interesting that I was glad to be able to praise Shostakovich. Asafyev laughingly remarked that I liked Shostakovich's piece so much because the first movement was quite clearly influenced by me . . .

After tea, the auditions resumed. First it was Deshevov's turn. Milhaud had praised him once after his Leningrad visit . . . Deshevov didn't want to leave the piano at all. He was as if obsessed with continuing with this and that, transcriptions for two and four hands. Meanwhile I was slowly getting impatient, as I wanted to hear the others too. It had grown late and my attention was beginning to wander.

Finally Deshevov was removed from the piano in a friendly way, and Popov took his place and played his Octet or Nonet.[209] . . . In the midst of the dense web of counterpoint one could undoubtedly discern a few interesting moments. Perhaps I would have discerned much more, had my head not been throbbing from all the music I had listened to . . . Flagging and impatient, I waited for the end of the Nonet and asked Sherbadchev to play something from his Sinfonietta, so that I could go home. But Sherbadchev intimated that I must hear a very interesting and well constructed organ piece by Kushnarev . . .

Meanwhile I was absolutely finished. Every sound felt like a glowing hot needle driven into my head. By the end of Kushnarev's piece I could not have stood another note. We said goodbye and left. Pity I never got to hear Sherbadchev's Sinfonietta . . .[210]

In Leningrad the composer participated in a performance of his opera *The Love for Three Oranges* in the presence of Lunacharsky. In Moscow he witnessed the first performance of his *Quintet*. He made plans with Meyerhold for new opera and ballet productions, and attended a conference on the future of the theatre where Meyerhold was the keynote speaker. Prokofiev's rehearsals and concerts were recorded on film. Banquets were held and countless newspaper articles appeared. Asafyev pointed to the need the country had for Prokofiev's music: 'Exactly the qualities which our contemporary music lacks, despite the good start it has made, have come together in this artist. His triumphal reception in Moscow is irrefutable proof that the creative spirit of his country, far from falling silent, has burst forth elementally in his passionate music.'[211] Only a few critical voices were raised to protest that, as one letter to the editor put it 'this fine musician emigrated from his country, which was becoming a society of workers and peasants, in a most cowardly and unseemly manner.'[212]

Prokofiev strenuously denied a newspaper report that he had applied to reactivate his Soviet citizenship: *Nonsense. There was nothing to reactivate. I was a Soviet citizen in 1918 when I departed, and I continue to be one now that I return.*[213] And indeed along with his international Nansen passport, Prokofiev also held a Soviet passport. He had had it endorsed at the Soviet embassy in Paris as early as 1924, after France's diplomatic recognition of the Soviet Union. Nestyev reported in the first version of his biography, which appeared in America in 1946, that: 'One of the first steps he took upon arrival in his homeland was to take out Soviet citizenship.'[214] The fact that this sentence no longer appears in the later Russian version of the biography, and the, suspicion that it had been 'suppressed'[215] there, enabled the assumption to take hold for many years that Prokofiev had lost his citizenship 'on the grounds of his long absence'.[216]

Despite the overwhelming impression made on him by his success, contact with friends, the country and the language, Prokofiev's personal interests and artistic milieu remained closely connected with the Western world. A special part was played in his struggle to come to grips with Soviet cultural and daily life by Diaghilev's new production of his ballet *Le Pas D'Acier*. The impresario had learned about Russian Constructivism from exhibitions and personal contacts with Mayakovsky in Berlin, and at a guest performance given by Alexander Tairov's chamber players in Paris. In it he saw in it a chance to impress the artistic world of Paris with a new idea once more. His plan to draw on the daily lives of workers and peasants in socialist Russia coincided to a considerable degree with Prokofiev's own artistic preoccupations. *I couldn't believe my ears. To me it was like a window letting in fresh air.*[217] For the libretto and the décor they were able to procure Georgi Yakulov, who had a great success as a producer both in the Soviet Union and in Paris. The artistic direction was taken on by Leonide Massine, after Tairov and Meyerhold had declined, as had the young soviet choreographer Kassian Goleisovski. *It was understood that under the circumstances it was not primarily a question of providing entertainment, but rather of creating a representation of the new world that was emerging in the Soviet Union, and above all of how it was being built. In our ballet there were to be hammers and piles, rotating flywheels and transmissions on the stage, along with coloured signals that lit up. All this was to culminate in a great creative surge, in which the dance troupe had simultaneously to work at the machine and symbolically represent the workings of the machines through dance.*[218]

Prokofiev tried to capture the mechanics of the machine age, *the language . . . of the present,*[219] through a stylistic reorientation of his music, with simple extensively diatonic melodies and austere pounding rhythms, but without eschewing sharp dissonances and shrill instrumentation. In June 1927 the Paris première of this ballet, hailed as 'a powerful new art form,'[220] created the expected sensation, with 'all Paris' in attendance: Picasso and Cocteau were present, Stravinsky and Ravel, Copland, Villa-Lobos, Nadia Boulanger and Vladimir Horovitz. The first performance in London the following month consolidated this success. 'The house, sold out to the last seat, applauded enthusiastically,' wrote the newspapers. 'Sergey Prokofiev deserves his fame. As an apostle of Bolshevism he has no peer.'[221]

On 19 August 1929 the death of Diaghilev brought an end to an epoch of Russian culture in the West, and also an end to its continuity from pre-Revolutionary avant-garde art. Even in the 1940s, when in the Soviet Union Diaghilev's name had long epitomized escapist decadence, Prokofiev paid emphatic tribute to his worth: *Over here his artistic activities have not yet been adequately acknowledged, and many are disposed to see him simply as an impresario who tapped real artists' brains. Yet his influence on art and especially his credit in propagandizing Russian art are enormous. Diaghilev would undoubtedly still be active on our behalf today, if he were still alive.*[222] Of course for Prokofiev personally,

Diaghilev portrait by Valentin Serov

Diaghilev's death and Koussevitzky's departure for the United States not long after severed important ties with the Western cultural scene.

Further planned trips to Russia failed to materialize, whether for 'technical reasons' as was said (the organizers could not commit themselves to paying Prokofiev's fee in foreign currency), or from artistic considerations (in the spring of 1928, after postponement of the production of *The Gambler* until the autumn and in December, after all plans to stage the opera had been finally abandoned). Later, political circumstances determined Prokofiev's temporizing attitude (as for instance after the protests by proletarian cultural organizations against the planned staging of *Le Pas D'Acier* in 1929, and later again after the politically motivated suicide of Mayakovsky in 1930).

Prokofiev's second trip to the Soviet Union from the end of October to November 1929 coincided with negotiations over the production of the ballet *Le Pas D'Acier* in Moscow. At first the Soviet press had welcomed the ballet as a cultural event. Lunacharsky, Asafyev and Meyerhold all commended the establishment of

Meyerhold, Shostakovich, Mayakovsky and Rodchenko in rehearsal

international artistic associations. Meyerhold himself wanted to take over the production. Introducing a Prokofiev concert on theatre radio, he tried to convince listeners of the enormous propaganda value of the ballet, and alluded to the composer's importance for the common cause of Russian music and the Revolution: 'Prokofiev's destiny has shaped itself in such a way that despite his desire to rejoin us, he is obliged to remain abroad for the time being in fulfilment of ongoing contracts. But although he lives in the West, the direction of his artistic productivity is nevertheless in complete accord with the epoch of great works . . . The underlying tone of his creative enterprise is perfectly attuned to our times. His work flows like a mighty river into modern Russian music, which is fundamentally different from Western European musical activity . . . Prokofiev is helping our cause in the West. He is our musical outpost.'[223] The Russian Association of Proletarian Musicians naturally registered its vigorous opposition. They objected that if the ballet had been acclaimed in the West as the work of a Bolshevik composer, that it represented a 'denigration of the Revolution'[224] and an anti-Soviet misrepresentation of the country from an outsider's point of view. The composer had to attend a hearing. After three concert performances, the planned production was scrapped.

By the end of the 1920s the era of innovative pluralism in Soviet art was substantially over. Under the aegis of the first 'Five-Year Plan', the proletarian associations were able to establish their profile and extend their influence. They sought to imprint the cultural atmosphere with the stamp of their simplifications and optimism. The dismissal of Lunacharsky from his post as Commissar for

Culture in 1929 was a clear signal. Prokofiev's ballet *Le Pas D'Acier*, Shostokovich's opera *The Nose*, (blamed among other things for being too much influenced by Prokofiev),[225] soon fell victim to the attacks of the Russian Association of Proletarian Musicians. In April 1930 Vladimir Mayakovsky, under growing ideological pressure, committed suicide. 'It is hard to imagine what might happen next,' Nikolay Myaskovsky warned his friend. 'At all events good music, especially contemporary music, and particularly Russian music, will have to be set aside for the present . . . Under the current circumstances, I don't think there is any point in your coming here.'[226] But Prokofiev was more than ever intent on acting as ambassador for Soviet music in the West. He played works by

The giants of Soviet music: Prokofiev, Shostakovich and Khachaturian, 1945

Myaskovsky, Shostakovich, Khachaturian, Shebalin, and Mossolov, organized recitals, and supported Russian composers through his contacts with Western conductors and publishers. He went to great lengths to arrange for Shostakovich to visit Paris.

At the same time, Stalin's new policy of 'offensive on all fronts', aimed at all interests of political, economic, and social systems, was having an increasing effect on cultural life. On 23 April 1932 the Central Committee of the Communist Party issued a resolution 'on the restructuring of literary and artistic organizations'. All associations were dissolved and replaced by monolithic artists' unions, among them the 'Central Soviet Union of Composers'. The aim and the declared rationale for resolution was the homogenization of Soviet cultural life and its integration into the fabric of the Communist Party. Maxim Gorky played a central role in this reshaping of Soviet cultural politics, and, most significantly helped formulate the guidelines for the doctrine of 'socialist realism'.

Dimitri Shostakovich (1906–1975). Shostakovich's family was originally Polish. His father was exiled to Siberia for his involvement in the Polish Revolt against Tsar Alexander II. In 1919, Shostakovich went to the Petrograd Conservatory, where he studied piano with Nikolayev and composition with Shteinberg. He had an unprecedented, worldwide success with his graduation work, his *First Symphony*, which was conducted in the United States by Toscanini and Bruno Walter. In 1927, his piano playing won him a prize at the Chopin competition in Warsaw. In 1937, he went to teach at the Moscow Conservatory. He embarked on an astonishing cycle of quartets, which were heavily influenced by the lucidity of Prokofiev's *Second Quartet*, and which completely re-awoke the century's faith in the message of the medium. No composer since Beethoven has more successfully used the quartet as confessional chronicle. In 1948, he was attacked alongside Prokofiev by Zhdanov, and his work was banned.

Unlike Prokofiev who was physically destroyed by the attacks, Shostakovich responded with sarcasm and private defiance. He wrote cinema music to pay the rent, and continued to write music 'for the desk'.

With the death of Stalin in 1953, he produced his most outspoken orchestral work, the *Tenth Symphony*, which included a vicious musical portrait of the dictator.

This not only forced artists to submit to a political programme, but also to a set of aesthetic maxims constituting a practical methodology. Socialist realism, repeatedly defined and delimited in eloquent debates, required art to be in harmony with a given historical, socialist reality by adopting a consensual positive attitude towards it. For music, the main requirement, as formulated by the critic Victor Gorodinski in *Soviet Music* (the journal of the Composers' Union), was a 'folk simplicity' and 'national bonding'.[227]

These new of cultural politics signalled an end to the exhausting disagreements between artists and extreme proletarian groups. Seen thus the resolutions, especially as they were connected with the name of Maxim Gorky, were initially quite welcome. It was Myaskovsky, with his *Twelfth Symphony*, called 'Kolchos', and later the 'October Symphony', who was one of the first to attempt to give musical expression to these new notions of official optimism and (non-abrasive) popular accessibility. Prokofiev, though crudely attacked the previous year by the Russian Association of Proletarian Musicians, which labelled him a 'White Guardist and Fascist',[228] now reconsidered the idea of returning. At the end of 1932 he set

Aram Khachaturian (1903–1974) was born in Tiflis (Tbilisi), in Georgia on the 6 June 1903, to Armenian parents. In 1922, he entered the biology department of Moscow University, whilst there he attended the famous Gnesin Music School. He studied composition with the school's famous founder, Mikhail Gnesin and from 1929 continued to study with him at the Moscow Conservatory. He later took lessons with Myaskovsky, and soon became his teaching assistant. He also studied with Dmitri Shostakovich. On the 10 February 1948, Khachaturian was condemned, alongside Shostakovich, Popov and Prokofiev as one of the principal offenders of a group 'guilty of following decadent, formalist western trends'. This attack was only finally amended by the central committee of the communist party in the May of 1958. From the 1950's onwards, he became deeply involved in work for the communist party, and the time that he spent on both his party work and conducting certainly distracted him from composition. He made much use of folk music in his writing, not only from his native Armenia, but also from the Caucasus and the Black Sea areas. He was married to the composer and conductor, Nina Markarova. He died of lung cancer in Moscow in 1974. His most successful works were those written for the great Soviet Virtuosi, particularly the *Violin Concerto*, which was popularised by Oistrakh, who wrote his own cadenza for it, his Piano Concerto, which became as popular as Prokofiev's, particularly in the US, and the cello concerto which he wrote for the indefatigable Rostropovich. By his judicious use of folk material, often left in original form, he was able to conceal the true originality of his writing behind an ingenuous surface. His neglected late works lay this veneer to one side, they are dry and challenging, particularly the extraordinary *Sonata-Monologue* for solo violin, written shortly before he died.

KHACHATURIAN

Prokofiev and Myaskovsky

out for his third concert tour in the Soviet Union. He aired his pro-posed move in discus-sions with representatives of the Educational Commissariat and the Composers' Union, and entered into negotia-tions with the Moscow Conserva-tory about taking up a part-time teaching position. By April 1933, after an extended tour of the United States, the composer was back in the Soviet Union. The intervals between his visits were becoming shorter and shorter. In conversation with Serge Moreaux in Paris in 1933, Prokofiev spoke about his firm intention of return-ing. *It is like this: foreign air is not conducive to my inspiration because I am Russian . . . I must go back. I must immerse myself in the atmosphere of my native land again. I must see real winters again, and the spring breaking forth from one moment to the next. I must hear the Russian language resonating in my ear again. I must talk to people who are of my own flesh and blood, so they can give me something in return which I don't have here; their songs, my songs. Here I am becoming enervated. I am in danger of succumbing to academicism. Yes, my friend, I am going back.*[229]

Nikolay Myaskovsky (1881–1950) studied with Glière from 1902–3. He joined Lyadov's composition class in 1906, at the comparatively late age of 25, and also, like Prokofiev and Stravinsky, studied with Rimsky-Korsakov. He met the young Prokofiev at the St Petersburg Conservatory, and the two remained close friends and corre-sponded extensively for the whole of their lives. He was the most prolific symphonist of Soviet Russia. His 13 String Quartets had an enormous impact on the chamber music of Shostakovich.

Shostakovich's opera *Lady Macbeth of the Mtsensk District* has become a key work in Soviet music, a symbol of the interweaving of music and politics, 'the first clear example of what Communist totalitarianism means in art'.[230] Shostakovich had tried to secure the reception of his work in various ways in a pre-emptive article, as dealing with the theme of women's plight in pre revolutionary Russia, with passing reference to Gorky, and as an ambivalent satire involving contempt for the 'petit bourgeois' classes.[231] He did not neglect to allude to musical developments since his last opera *The Nose*,

Joseph Stalin

and the current preference for singable tunes. The opera, first performed in 1934, became an exceptional success, celebrated as a sensational masterpiece in the West, and extolled in the Soviet press a 'the great proletarian opera'.[232] Then quite unexpectedly came the now familiar verdict. In January 1936 Stalin attended two guest performances by the Leningrad Theatre in Moscow: *Quiet flows the Don* by Ivan Dzerzhinsky and Shostakovich's *Lady Macbeth of the Mtsensk District*. With the same decisiveness that he welcomed the idyllic realism and pompous display of Dzerzhinsky's work, Stalin rejected the directness and satirical bite of Shostakovich's drama about adultery, murder, greed, passion, destruction, and self-annihilation: 'Stalin found the opera objectionable.'[233] On 28 January an unprecedented article appeared in the Communist Party organ *Pravda*, attacking Shostakovich's opera as 'Chaos instead of music.' The opera was immediately removed from the scheduled programmes of all Soviet theatres. It was endlessly discussed in regional meetings of the Composers' Union and the press. Explanations were submitted.[234]

Shostakovich had been singled out as a prominent example. But

Sergey and Lina Prokofiev in America

fundamental issues were at stake, questions about 'Modernism,' 'Naturalism' and 'Formalism' in art, and how literature and theatre should be conceived. In February 1936 the Central Congress of Composers reiterated and clarified the complaints against Shostakovich. Other composers fell under 'suspicion of formalism', Alexander Mossolov, Gabriel Popov and Henry Litinski, as well as various musicologists, including Ivan Sollertinski, the last Schoenberg apologist, in the Soviet Union, until the rise of Webern's student Hershkowitz in the 1970s. Asafyev, who, from initially being a 'Modernist' had by then become a celebrated composer of socialist realist ballets, tried to deflect attention away from Shostakovich as a person. In an official report he described the 'exciting questions' that had arisen as a general 'problem in the musical development of the Soviet Union'.[235]

During all of this Prokofiev was on concert tour in Europe, celebrated as both pianist and conductor and ever wider as an established composer. In March 1936 he returned to Moscow.

In May 1936 Prokofiev, with his wife Lina and their two sons Sviatoslav and Oleg, took up permanent residence in the Soviet Union. Prokofiev's return to Russia, his final and voluntary decision in favour of this country during what was certainly one of the darkest chapters of its history, has met with little retrospective understanding. Stravinsky, who thought the move stupid, ascribed pecuniary motives to the composer's desire to relocate: 'He followed the bitch goddess success, nothing else. He had had no luck in the

United States and Europe for several years, whereas his visit to Russia became a triumphal parade. When I saw him last in 1939 in New York, he was quite desperate about his financial and artistic fortunes in France. He was politically naïve ... and by the time he fully understood the situation over there, it was too late.'[236]

Prokofiev's circumstances in the West were certainly not 'desperate'. Interest in his personality and his work was undiminished. His music was performed with great success. And the publication of new works by Koussevitzky's press, together with income from frequently performed works such as the *Classical Symphony* or the *Third Piano Concerto*, ensured his financial independence. And just before his return to the Soviet Union the composer had received 'in every respect an attractive offer'[237] from an American university. In fact, unlike Stravinsky, Prokofiev had never been considered a composer of the very first rank in Europe. By contrast, from his first visit to the Soviet Union he was billed as the 'most frequently played among living composers'.[238] Despite this, even the overwhelming success of his music in the Soviet Union was not the ultimate reason for Prokofiev's return. 'Like a true Russian,' according to the recollections of his son Sviatoslav, 'he was homesick for Russia. Whenever he

Prokofiev and Lina with their sons Sviatoslav and Oleg, 1936

went to give concerts in the Soviet Union to enormous acclaim, he would get together with many of his old friend well, and new friends are not the same as old friends'.[239]

Nicolas Nabokov, who was on more intimate terms with the composer personally than Stravinsky, believed that he had problems with the new Soviet world, and many misgivings in the wake of the attack on Shostakovich.[240] However, Prokofiev's personal freedom was initially untouched. The privileges he enjoyed were unusual, even for prominent citizens. His lifestyle set him apart from all his colleagues, and was frequently interpreted as a sign of pretentiousness and arrogance. In fact, Prokofiev and his wife showed little sensitivity towards a Russia burdened with 'Five-Year Plans', or the impression their privileged status and luxuries were making, whether it were enquiries for American books and elegant clothing, or their children's education at an international diplomatic school, or the purchase of a particularly comfortable home, or, interestingly enough, the purchase of a motorcar which Prokofiev had shipped especially from the United States.

Prokofiev's links to the West remained unbroken. At the end of 1936 the composer again left the Soviet Union for a concert tour through Western Europe and the United States. On a further extended tour in 1938 he reestablished contact with his colleagues in France, especially with Stravinsky and Milhaud, and met up with Arnold Schoenberg in Hollywood.[241] At this point the composer could persuade himself that he was now leading an active international life from Moscow, much as he formerly had from Paris. However, it was to be Prokofiev's last sojourn abroad. Future travel requests would all be turned down. Yet, even without his personal mediation, Prokofiev's music continued to enjoy undiminished esteem in the West, where his popularity increased unabated.

From the outset Prokofiev had been prepared to collaborate in the reorganization of state and society, as much as it lay in his power as artist and musician. As early as 1933 he had accepted a three-year teaching assignment in the master classes of the Moscow Conservatory. Here he was able to observe his enormous influence on young Soviet composers. He curtailed his concert activities to make time for composing. And he tried to play his political part as a Soviet composer. He studied Lenin's writings with an eye to their import for musical composition. He also accepted commissions from Soviet film organizations, from the Moscow Theatre and

Pan-Union Radio. He took part in competitions, both as a jury member and as a composer, for marches and popular songs, on the theme of the relationship between daily life and work. Prokofiev had entered popular songs for the first time in 1933 in a contest organized by *Pravda*, among them his prize winning *Anyutka*. To get a sense of the scale of these competitions, one needs to look at the figures: 4,500 literary and 2,000 musical compositions were submitted, around 400 tunes alone for Golodny's *Partisan Shelsnyak*. Prokofiev's contributions, supplemented by other songs, appeared in 1935 as *Six Songs* Op 66. Further popular songs were collected in *Songs of our Time* for solos, mixed choir, and orchestra. Prokofiev also contributed to the social life of the Soviet Union with instrumental pieces, such as the *Spartacus March* for wind orchestra or the *Symphonic Overture on Russian Themes* for quadruple orchestral accompaniment.

In November 1937 the first of the 'Soviet Music Festivals' celebrating the twentieth anniversary of the October Revolution was held, with an array of significant first performances. The central event was the first performance of Shostakovich's *Fifth Symphony*, the 'musical answer to justified criticism'[242] which completely rehabilitated the composer. Myaskovsky presented his *Sixteenth* and *Eighteenth Symphonies* to the public, and an entire concert was devoted to Prokofiev, featuring the *Fourth Symphony*, the *Second Violin Concerto* and the second suite from *Romeo and Juliet*. As a special contribution to the festival, Prokofiev composed *Cantata to the 20th Anniversary of the October Revolution*, his attempt at a large-scale work in the official 'political' style. The texts, which appear in the chronological order of the historical events themselves, were taken from articles and speeches by Marx, Engels, Lenin, and Stalin. Protesting his loyalty in *Pravda* the composer tried to generate interest in his work and draw attention to himself: *The main themes of the work are the great socialist October Revolution itself, the victory, the industrializing of the country and the constitution. The cantata is written for two choirs, one professional the other lay, and for four orchestras, a symphony orchestra, a woodwind orchestra, a percussion orchestra and an accordion. No fewer than 500 people are required. I wrote this piece with great enthusiasm. The exceptional events with which it is associated also required an exceptional musical language. But I hope its vehemence and forthrightness will make it accessible to our listeners.*[243] However, the composer was unable to communicate his enthusiasm. The official music critics slated this homage to Stalinist giganticism as a less than successful experiment. The work was neither performed nor published during Prokofiev's lifetime.

On 21 December 1939 the Soviet Union celebrated Stalin's sixtieth birthday with a chorus of panegyrics to the dictator in speeches, poems, and music. Prokofiev conveyed his congratulations in his not unimpressive, *Toast to Stalin,* setting texts drawn from contemporary folksongs; Russian, Ukrainian, Belorussian, Kurdish, Marian and Mordvinian. This music was played 'over all the loudspeakers through the streets and squares of Moscow', Oleg Prokofiev recalls. 'It sounded unusually loud and desolate in the broad empty Chkalov Street where we were living at that time. Winter, the wind driving the snowflakes over the dark gloomy asphalt, not a soul on the street and the folk choir droning away in those strange harmonies.'[244]

Despite all his efforts to achieve recognition by working in the officially approved 'mass genres' – songs, cantatas, marches and other forms of utilitarian music – Prokofiev was never appreciated as much as he had hoped. As so often again later, he was criticized for his epic melodies and his prosaic recitatives. Indeed the intensity of the portrayal of the Revolution in his *Cantata,* which rolls together all available vocal and instrumental resources, evoking battle sounds and cannonades, alarm bells and wailing sirens, shows distinct affinities with the cataclysmic finale of *The Fiery Angel.*

Repeatedly Prokofiev resorted to words to publicize his views. In a series of articles written between 1932 and 1937 he tried to influence the *direction Soviet music*[245] was taking. Early on, he recognized the *not inconsiderable danger for today's Soviet composers of losing themselves in provincialism.*[246] He repeatedly vouched for the open-mindedness of the working public towards new music: *all these pseudo-folksy works which are largely in bad taste should be avoided.*[247]

The days when music was written for a small circle of aesthetes are gone. Now large masses of the people stand face to face with serious music, questioning and waiting . . . But this does not mean this audience should be pandered to. Conciliatoriness has an element of dishonesty about it, and nothing good ever came of that. The masses . . . understand considerably more than some composers think.[248]

We must recognize where we lag behind and catch up. This is something that should be considered by our composers who try to progress using the 'techniques of yesterday', yet sometimes don't even master these. We all have gifts. However, our gifted young people should not go forward by the way of least resistance, but rather that of greatest fulfilment.[249]

Formalism, he boldly objected after the debate about *Lady Macbeth of the Mtsensk District, is sometimes with us what is not understood immediately.*[250] And he pleaded rationally for leave to also write contemporary music in the Soviet Union using a modern language: *The quest for a musical idiom appropriate to the Socialist epoch is not an easy task for the composer but it is an honourable one. Music in our country has become the property of the masses. Their artistic tastes, and the demands they make on art, are growing with truly incredible speed. It is imperative that with each new work Soviet composers keep an eye on these continuing developments lest they be left behind . . . For this reason I consider all attempts at simplification by a composer wrong-headed . . . In the works that I have written during this creatively profitable year, I have tried to achieve a clear and melodious idiom. At the same time I have not been in the least concerned to deck myself out with stale harmonic and melodic turns of phrase. The difficulty lies in composing in a clear musical language, while recognizing that this clarity must be not the old one but a new one.*[251]

Composer in the Soviet Union

Two works are particularly highly regarded by Soviet music historians as evidence of a stylistic change of direction in Prokofiev's work: the ballet music *Romeo and Juliet* and the *Second Violin Concerto*. These works, according to Nestyev, reflect a rejection of the 'Directionlessness of his composing'[252] after his return to the Soviet Union.

Prokofiev explicitly dissociated his *Second Violin Concerto*, composed in 1935, from his first work in this genre written nearly twenty years earlier. *As regards both form and content I wanted to do something completely different.*[253] The layout and sequence of the movements, fast-slow-fast, are in established traditional form. These movements themselves utilize conventional 19th-century harmonic structures. The orchestral part is lightly scored; even at the (loud) end of the piece only half of the orchestra is actually playing, and the virtuoso element in the solo part is apparently conventionally developed: rapidly ascending scales, staccato and spiccato configurations, sequential chains of double-stops and arpeggios. On closer examination, however, the intricate articulation and subtle syntax of this figuration is revealed to be enriched by a labyrinth of mathematical sleights of hand and isometric games. Perhaps, like many composers at this time, Prokofiev was finding ways of incorporating the intellectual rigour of Schoenbergs's ideas of number and structural integration, whilst eschewing serialism itself. The cantabile sections also conform to received notions of 'spiritedness': the introduction of the second subject using clarinets, horns, and bass strings, the almost clichéd enchantment of the romantic vocalize of the solo violin against pizzicato groundwork by the orchestra in the slow middle movement. This lyricism, and its relationship to the compositional structure of the piece, is a long way from the bizarre and aggressive contrasts of Prokofiev's *First Violin Concerto*.

Nevertheless Prokofiev did not write the *Second Violin Concerto* as music for the Soviet Union at all. This move toward the romantic-bourgeois concept of the solo concerto has more to do with the genesis of the work as a piece commissioned for a specific person. Prokofiev wrote it for the French violinist Robert Soetens, who received sole performance rights for a whole year; another work regarded as a major Soviet achievement is Prokofiev's ballet *Romeo and Juliet*, one of his most popular compositions, an enduring success in both East and West. But the work made its way on to the stage in the Soviet Union after a long and tortuous process. The work originated in connection with the Shakespeare cult which had continued to make its mark on Soviet cultural life since the 1930s.[254] In the autumn of 1934 Prokofiev jumped at the proposal made by the ballet theatres in Leningrad and Moscow that he should write his music for a full evening of ballet on 'Romeo and Juliet'. Sergey Radlov, who as early as 1926 had been entrusted with the Leningrad première of *The Love for Three Oranges*, undertook to prepare a libretto in collaboration with the composer. Just one year later the music was complete. However, the commissioning theatres were not prepared to go along with the fluidity of Prokofiev's music. The work was controversial in many ways. Not only was the novel plan of changing the final scene, having the lovers re-awakening and dancing joyfully, rejected, but the music was received with overwhelming scepticism. It was widely regarded as too complicated to dance, the abrupt and continually changing rhythms as running counter to the needs of ballet. Rehearsals were postponed. And so it was the Czech dancer and choreographer Ivo Váňa Psotas who first staged *Romeo and Juliet* in Brunn in 1938.[255] Admittedly, this production made so little impression that much later Soviet music

ROMEO AND JULIET

historians referred to the long-awaited Leningrad performance in 1940 as the première.[256] This, with choreography by Leonid Lavrovsky and Pyotr Williams' décor, was received with frenetic enthusiasm by both audience and critics. To this day it is recognized as one of the shining achievements of Soviet musical theatre.

The success of this production, however, was based on a misunderstanding. Even later Prokofiev was not much disposed to share the generally favourable judgements of Lavrovsky (whose staging often ran counter to the music).[257] Lavrovsky's heavy pathos and illusionistic translation of the love tragedy into a welter of decorative details, 'folksy' purple passages, and melodramatic exaggeration were all in marked contrast to Prokofiev's vision of a panorama of contrasting perspectives and counterpointed lighting. Prokofiev's notion of introducing a 'happy ending' should also be understood as germane to the strategy of breaking away from illusionistic theatre. The aim was not to arouse psychologically coherent emotions of sympathy for a fateful sequence of tragic complications, but rather to give a frankly theatrical presentation of absurd events: 'this is not the way things should have happened.' [258]

1936 was also the year of Prokofiev's intensive involvement as a composer with Alexander Pushkin. The impending centenary of the poet's death was publicized the length and breadth of the country: there were Pushkin performances and films, plus an array of scholarly publications and artistic tributes. Prokofiev contributed to three such projects. He wrote the music for Mikhail Romm's film *The Queen of Spades*, as well as incidental music for the stage productions *Eugene Onegin* at the Moscow Chamber Theatre and *Boris Gudonov* at Meyerhold's theatre. *Of these three works 'Eugene Onegin' interested me most. In the production of 'Eugene Onegin' by S S Krishishanovski it is especially the moments in Pushkin's poem that are disregarded in Tchaikovsky's opera that are brought out . . . As is well known, opinions about Tchaikovsky's opera, have been divided. Some have regarded the composer's adaptation as an unqualified success, others have felt that*

Tchaikovsky took the fire out of Pushkin and replaced it with his own pessimism. I personally set myself the goal of penetrating as far as possible to the true spirit of Pushkin.[259]

Tchaikovsky's opera is a sad romantic story, 'lyrical scenes', as he himself described them set against a realistic backdrop of the Russian salons. In contrast Prokofiev's music preserves Pushkin's detachment from his hero. Onegin's ennui and melancholy, Tatyana's unworldliness, and Lenski's sentimentalities do not dissolve into lyrical effusions. They are analytically and critically accompanied. Prokofiev counterposes a deeper awareness of the characters to Tchaikovsky's emotional infatuation. Predominantly textless, the music falls into twenty-five short sections accompanying Pushkin's verses word for word. The varied development of leitmotifs highlights relationships, foreshadows coming events and guides the listener's reactions. In its dramatic effectiveness, Prokofiev's scores may be favourably compared to his film music.

The composer's passion for this poet reflects a certain spiritual affinity between them. This may be said to reside in a mutual balance between controlled clarity and lightly ironic intonation, between laconic detachment and spontaneity whilst playing artistically with double meanings, between contrasts of romantic and realistic elements. In the event, not one of the Pushkin projects could be implemented. The fact that *all the music . . . remained unused,* however, did not occur *through the fault of the theatres,*[260] Prokofiev maintained. Politically motivated criticism, perhaps because of Meyerhold's portrayal of the roots of autocratic tyranny, was a more decisive factor. (Prokofiev's apportioning of blame, especially in an article which in other respects shows no sign of opportunism, is bound to appear somewhat cynical in view of Meyerhold's fate.[261]) Prokofiev later made use of the material in the scores for his other Pushkin works.[262] His only published compositions for the Pushkin centenary were the *Three Romances* Op 73. These are songs that explicitly turn their back on the prosaic style of the early

Akhmatova and Balmont songs. Sentimental and conventional, they perfectly reflect the sensitive romantic modalities of the previous century.

Prokofiev's project, the following spring, was very much in compliance with contemporaneous cultural and political requirements, a model of the didactic application of socialist realism to music. In the West, even today, it is still the composer's best-known and best-loved work, a popular and enduringly successful classic: *Peter and the Wolf, a Symphonic Children's Fairy Tale* for narrative voice and orchestra. Here Prokofiev responded to the encouragement of Natalia Satz, the artistic director of the Central Children's Theatre in Moscow.[263] He did not like the text the poet Nina Saksonskaya proposed for his

Prokofiev plays while Natalia Satz reads
Peter and the Wolf in Moscow, 1936

composition. Prokofiev's own text is in prose and using language typical of him – direct, dry, and laconic. In his foreword the composer highlighted the pedagogical objective of the work. *Every active person in this fairy tale is represented in the orchestra by one or more instruments: the little bird by the flute, the duck by the oboe, the cat by the bass clarinet (staccato), the grandfather by the bassoon, the wolf by chords on the French horns, Peter by the string instruments, the huntsman's shots by the large and kettle drums. The idea is to show these instruments to the children before the performance and to demonstrate the leitmotifs. In this way they learn to distinguish a whole range of instruments during the performance without the slightest effort.*[264]

Interpretations of what Prokofiev's fairy-tale means continue to vary greatly. Interestingly enough, Asafyev praised the realistic presentation of the action as conforming with social realist demands for typicality and universal validity: 'What could be more everyday! than young Peter's experiences in the fairy-tale *Peter and the Wolf*? Yet in the music everything sounds as though it were happening for the first time ever upon earth. Every detail of the behaviour of the boy, the duck, the little bird, the cat, and the wolf sounds new. One wonders whether elements of the new Soviet symphonic spirit cannot be detected here, liberated now from all the intellectual's individualistic self-analysis, along with all subjective interpretations of reality.'[265] Nestyev commented on it simply as a 'naïve story'.[266] Harlow Robinson, author of the most recent and best informed Prokofiev biography, put forward a socially subversive interpretation: the grandfather is the embodiment of rigid establishment opinion, parents, grandparents, the party, against which a revolt is not only intelligent but likely to succeed.[267] Prokofiev himself publically explained the story as a timely parable: 'Pioneer Petya', as the hero is called in the Russian original, personifies the bold, forward-looking Soviet Union fighting against the greedy capitalist world, specifically Hitler's Germany: *Pioneers like him are not afraid of wolves.*

If the 1920s in both the East and West were marked by experimentation in all the arts under the banner of the avant-garde, the 1930s led to a fresh re-alignment with traditional values. In the field of opera, along with Schoenberg's *Moses and Aaron*, Křenek's *Charles V* or Hindemith's *Mathis der Maler*, confessional operas on universal topics drawn from mythology and history started to appear.[268] To Soviet opera composers, especially after the events surrounding Shostakovich's *Lady Macbeth of the Mtsensk District*, the quest for subject matter that embraced everyday realities presented itself as a question about the nature of socialist reality. Prokofiev's road to artistic and social responsibility as a Soviet composer was marked by his commitment to socially relevant operatic themes: *What sort of subject am I looking for? Not a caricature of shortages, of the external imperfections of our daily life. At the present point in time that does not appeal to me. I am looking for a subject which takes a positive approach to things, an Eroica of national construction.*[269]

On Alexey Tolstoy's advice, Prokofiev turned to a story by

Valentin Katayev, *I am a Son of the Working People*. In this tale, which is as conventional as it is didactic, Katayev portrays the political situation in the Ukraine after the Revolution: *Love between young people, hatred of the representatives of the old order, militant heroism, lamentation over what has been lost, and typical Ukrainian humour.*[270] Prokofiev changed the tendentious title, but tried nonetheless to accommodate Party directives requiring idealized portrayal of the Soviet people's heroism. His opera *Semyon Kotko* is a transitional work. The composer could not share Katayev's vision of a folk opera with dance interludes and songs in rhyme, something light and cheerful in mood with a clear political message. His prose-like music is essentially melodic recitative, with a fragmented structure constructed from short cinematic episodes, but still well in advance of his later reversion to the traditional operatic conventions of recitatives and arias, choruses and ensemble. For all its striving after a realistic portrayal of the present, Prokofiev's expressive idiom shows evidence of musical self-reliance and political courage. The director of the first production was to be Meyerhold. Increasingly Meyerhold's ideas on the conscious autonomy of practical theatre were coming up against Stalinist demands for decorative stage realism. On 16 January 1939, at the national convention of theatre directors, he gave a speech on matters of principle. In the West this speech, as transmitted by the émigré violinist Yuri Yelagin, has become a symbol of fearlessness and refusal to be broken, a memorial to selfless commitment to art and freedom of expression.[271] It has been shown that the wording in Yelagin's document was tampered with. Meyerhold was thinking rather more about how to maintain his artistic convictions intact in the face of Stalinist cultural politics.[272] His wife, the actress Zinaida Raikh, was found murdered in their apartment shortly after his arrest, and within a year the director himself was shot in prison as a 'Trotskyite activist'.[273] The official report of the convention made no mention of Meyerhold, and his name disappeared for many years from the consciousness of Soviet art historians.[274]

Did Prokofiev know about Meyerhold's fate? There is certainly no evidence of his having used his international status to intercede on behalf of his endangered friend. Later his son Oleg remembered that 'a week before completion of the piano version of the opera, Meyerhold was arrested, and Prokofiev was left with the opera they had worked on in detail together, denied the strong hand of this remarkable director. I emphasize this point because if Meyerhold had staged the opera the confusion and the humiliating changes I myself witnessed at the rehearsals would probably have been avoided.'[275] The first production of the opera *Semyon Kotko* in 1940 sparked off a vigorous but remarkably open aesthetic discussion. Critics of the opera, who saw it as a reversion to the modernism Prokofiev had so publicly rejected eventually gained the upper hand, and it was not until the 1960s that the work reappeared in the repertoire of Soviet theatres.

The disappeared. Vsevolod Meyerhold stands before the portrait of his wife Zinaida Raikh

In 1941 the Soviet Union was suddenly at war. Konstantin Simonov, describing the German invasion of 22 June in his novel *The Living and the Dead*, observed that 'Everyone had been expecting the war, but despite this its outbreak came like a bolt out of the blue.'[276] By autumn Kiev had fallen, Leningrad was blockaded and Moscow was besieged. Winter, and Hitler's fatal miscalculation of the distances involved and the harsh conditions at that time of year brought the German invasion to a standstill. Stalin talked of the failure of Hitler's 'Blitzkrieg' and succeeded in mobilizing all

GERMAN INVASION

the country's resources, human, material, and moral to continue the war. The Great Patriotic War, which left twenty million dead and millions more wounded, has become a legend in the annals of Soviet history. The tragic memories of heroism and patriotism endure. It was a fight, Shostakovich remembers, 'for the best ideals in the history of mankind . . . , for everything we have created and built up'.[277] Shostakovich's *Seventh Symphony*, the 'Leningrad Symphony', performed in 1942 in the still besieged city of Leningrad, became the musical symbol of Soviet heroism.

Shortly after the first attacks, a government decree ordered the evacuation of the main cultural institutions from Moscow and Leningrad. Theatres, orchestras and conservatories, the furnishings of the Composers' Union, the main film studios, and a large number of artists were evacuated from the threatened cities. Prokofiev found himself in transit for two years, from Nalchik in the Caucasus via Tiflis in Georgia to Alma-Ata in Kazakhstan. The composer interrupted work on his ballet *Cinderella* and on preparations for the performance of his new comic opera *Betrothal in a Monastery* to devote more time to patriotic tasks. *The entire Soviet people rose up in defence of the country. Everyone wanted to contribute his bit immediately. The reaction of composers to events was naturally to produce songs and marches of a heroic character, that is, the kind of music that could be used at the front at once. I wrote two songs and one march.*[278] Along with these he produced the programmatic suite *The Year for the Friendship of all Peoples 1941* with movements titled 'Night', 'In Battle', and 'Ballad of the Unknown Child'. This cantata, based on a poem by Pavel Antokolsky. A child's revenge on the Nazis, for the murder of his family is described in expressive language and stark musical colouring. *My music tries to capture the dramatic spirit of the text and to make the cantata itself dramatic and forward-looking. As I composed it, I kept the disrupted childhood, the gruesome enemy, the unyielding courage and the shining victory near at hand all vividly before my mind's eye.*[279] Prokofiev also wrote political occasional music during the ensuing war years, and he participated in a competition for the national anthem of the USSR. How little suited Prokofiev's style of composing was to the idiom of politically motivated music is shown even by his *March for Military Orchestra*, which in 1944 was broadcast as part of the May Day festivities. The pared-down harmonic modulations and the technical difficulties for the performers alike make the work suitable for the concert hall but not for military use.

The contemporary situation is also reflected in Prokofiev's main work of the period, the opera *War and Peace*. Tolstoy's epic novel was considered an exemplary model for Soviet narrative realism. Among the contributing factors here was its projection of a broadly optimistic, forward-looking outlook on life, even in times of crisis. Tolstoy's antithetical principle of construction readily lent itself to episodic adaptation as an opera libretto: 'War and Peace . . . is not a novel, even less a poem, and less still a historical chronicle. *War and Peace* is what the author wanted to and was able to express in the form it took to express it.'[280] The novel's continual changes in location, contrasting scenes, and shifts in mood were features Prokofiev and his co-librettist Mira Mendelson found useful when it came to condensing and organizing autonomous scenes, alternating war and private life, epic and lyric, history and fiction. The material was divided into a total of seventy-two different roles, integrated musically through an intricate network of leitmotifs, reprises, and recapitulations. Formally, even though division into acts has been dispensed with, the link back to traditional opera with its arias, ensembles and choruses is plain. Moreover, the text does not follow its literary prototype as closely as, for instance, Prokofiev's earlier Dostoevsky opera *The Gambler*. Additional sources have been drawn upon, over and above the novel – letters, poems, maxims, and contemporaneous songs.

Prokofiev continued to work on this piece until the end of his life, shaping, completing, and revising. There is no definitive version of the opera. The history of its genesis and of its production overlap.

Dmitri Kabalevsky (1904–1987) was born in St Petersburg. When he was fourteen years old, his family moved to Moscow, where he attended the Skryabin Music School, where he studied composition with Gregory Catoire. He went on to the Conservatory at the age of twenty-one, to study composition with Myaskovsky and piano with Alexander Goldenweiser, who had been a close friend of Tolstoy. He taught as an instructor at the Conservatory from 1932. He wrote an enormous amount of pedagogical music, and thousands of young violinists worldwide have made their entrée into playing Russian music through his *Violin Concerto*. In 1962, in recognition of his educational work, he was made the head of the Commission for Musical Aesthetic Education of Children. This work received international recognition in 1972, when he was made honorary president of the International Society of Music Education. As the chief editor of *Soviet Music* in the late 1940s, his was the voice of party policy in music. His music succeeded in satisfying Stalin's most proscriptive demands, and avoiding the artistic terror unleashed by Zhdanov from 1948, whilst remaining of high quality; his was a fine melodic gift. He collaborated with Rostropovich on the completion of Prokofiev's *Concertino*, which was eventually premièred in 1960, and officiated at Prokofiev's funeral obsequies in 1953, the same year that Vladimir Ashkenazy premièred his *Third Piano Concerto*, under the composer's baton.

Suggestions for changes were already coming in from official quarters immediately work on it had ended in 1943. Their official objections had to do in the first instance with the predominance of the lyrical component. And considering that a patriotic war against Germany was raging, Prokofiev could hardly disregard their directive that he strengthen the dramatic and heroic aspects and shorten the genre scenes. *The parts that were moved into the foreground were specifically those depicting the Russian people's fight against Napoleon's hordes in 1812 and the expulsion of his army from Russian territory. It was evident that these were the aspects of the material that would have to form the mainstay of the opera.*[281]

In fact Prokofiev was attempting to communicate with the public, with the contemporary Soviet public. His desire to have the opera (which he regarded as his most important work) performed was extremely intense. He remarked to Dmitri Kabalevsky that he *was prepared to accept the fate of every one of my works, but if you only knew how important it is to me that 'War and Peace' should see the light of day.*[282] Mira Mendelson reported that even at the very end of his life he would talk almost daily about the possibility of having his work produced: 'He was incessantly preoccupied with the idea.'[283] It is the tragedy of the composer's late years that the whole project of his opera should sink beneath the wheels of Stalinist censorship. Prokofiev did not live to see a complete production.

'Of all the arts Film is for us the most important.'[284] Lenin's discovery of film as a vehicle for propaganda was of the utmost significance for the development of artistic modes of expression in this medium. Even today Soviet film from the pre-war period is surrounded by a kind of mystic aura. The left-wing avant-garde, the circle of Sergey Eisenstein and Vsevolod Pudovkin, represented a final revolutionary explosion in art,[285] and attracted the interest of the leading composers to film. And it was specifically in this field that, even in the 1930s, Soviet music could still count on inter-national attention. Prokofiev's contributions to film were all composed for Soviet productions between 1932 and 1946. They played a significant part in his process of finding an identity as a 'Soviet composer'. After his death they were correspondingly important in establishing his role as the 'national composer'.

Lieutenant Kijé (1933), Prokofiev's music for Alexander Fain-zimmer's film version of the novella by Yury Tynianov, reflected the influence of his earlier life shuttling between Paris and Moscow. Prokofiev's classicizing tendencies and his musical penchant for ironic and satirical effects were especially well suited to Tynianov's wry parody of the Tsarist bureaucratic world at the end of the 18th century. At the same time the film as a mass medium neatly com-plements the composer's endeavour to find *a musical language appro-priate to Soviet life,*[286] *a new simplicity, 'lightly serious' or 'seriously light'.*[287]

Prokofiev's collaboration with Eisenstein, the leading figure in Soviet film, has become legendary. After the masterpieces of the 1920s (*Strike, Battleship Potemkin, October*), his work had run into artistic difficulties. The constructive freedom and autonomy of his specific concepts of montage, the rapid free-floating juxtaposition of richly metaphorical sequences of images, were criticized as too intellectual and remote from reality. Eisenstein's first sound film, *Alexander Nevsky*, was a historical epic, made in 1938 as a political commission. The hero, Prince Novgorod, who led his troops to victory over the Knights of the German Order on the frozen ice of Lake Peipus, was as well suited to Stalin's aim of rehabilitating nationalism as it was to reflecting the historical preoccupations of the moment. 'Patriotism, that is my theme,' wrote Eisenstein, 'we have taken a historical event from the 13th century, when the Livonian and Teutonic Knights, the forerunners of today's Fascists, waged a systematic war of conquest in the East, and attempted to subject the Slavs and other peoples in the same way Fascist Germany is doing today, with the same angry slogans and the same fanaticism.'[288] The images from the past became a parable for the events of the present and the lesson of history became a political appeal. The

Sergey Eisenstein (1898–1948). No film-maker before or since has shown a greater understanding for music than Sergey Mikhailovich Eisenstein. After the Civil War he became the set designer at the Proletkult Theatre and studied with Meyerhold. He then turned to cinema, where he developed his interest in the use of combined characters in Japanese calligraphy into the first fully developed and practical theories of 'montage'. He first achieved fame with his silent film, *The Battleship Potemkin* in 1925. After making *October*, he left the Soviet Union in 1928, and directed, without marked success, in France, the United States and Mexico. On his return to the Soviet Union in 1932, he fell foul of the emergence of the 'socialist realist' doctrine. His collaboration with Prokofiev on *Alexander Nevsky*, released in 1939, returned him to favour and won the Order of Lenin. Between 1942 and 1946, he worked on a trilogy based on the life of Ivan the Terrible. On its release, the first part won him the Stalin Prize, but the dictator disapproved of part two; it was not released in their lifetimes. The final film in the trio was never made. Although he completed only six films before his death in 1948, he is considered one of the most influential filmmakers and film theoreticians of the 20th century.

clarity of Eisenstein's statement here underlies the unity and dramatic effectiveness of the film, the import of which is well expressed in the richly suggestive final words of the Novgorod Prince: 'He who comes to us with the sword shall perish by the sword.'

Prokofiev endeavoured to bring his music into perfect harmony with Eisenstein's images and text. *Film is a young, highly contemporary art form and it offers completely new and interesting opportunities to composers that must be exploited. Composers should go after them and not restrict themselves to simply composing music, and then leave it to a film company and the discretion of some sound-mixer as to how it should be used, as they may have the best of intentions but are not in a position to deal with the music as well as the composer himself.*[289] And conversely Eisenstein with his typical intuitiveness recognized the functional interdependence of music: *His reverence for music was so great that in some cases he was willing to extend or shorten the film's visual dimensions in order to keep the musical image intact.*[290]

Eisenstein and Prokofiev's concept of fully integrating the music into the drama operates on several levels. Realistic elements are introduced associatively: drum and trumpet signals are immediately echoed in the images, as is the Novgorods' song 'People of Russia Arise'. On another level, Prokofiev's music underscores the typecasting of characters as paradigms of either good or evil. Here the composer took advantage of the technical possibilities of sound recording as a mode of expression. Sound manipulation, distortions and sound effects achieved by placing the instruments close to the microphone, constitute the acoustic counterpart of Eisenstein's images of the German knights, images of 'an impersonal, soulless machine', of an 'avalanche of iron battering rams'.[291] The lively faces of the Russian people by contrast are echoed by original folk melodies. These quite different elements in the music are not self-explanatory; but their meaning emerges in counterpoint to the image. Prokofiev was fully convinced of the primacy of his own contemporary musical idiom in following the contours of the film,

COMPOSER FOR FILM

despite its historical subject-matter. *It is a real temptation to use the music handed down from those times. But even a cursory examination of the Catholic songs of the 13th century brings home the fact that in the course of seven centuries this music has become so remote from us, so alien to us in feeling, that it is no longer capable of providing the audience's imagination with sufficient sustenance. It therefore seemed considerably more 'advantageous' not to present it as it really would have sounded at the time of the battle on the ice, but rather in a form we can imagine it happening today. The same went for the Russian song, which had to assume a contemporary guise, and the question of how it would have been sung seven hundred years ago was set aside.*[292] Strictly non-musical events are also transposed into music by the use of leitmotifs. In the battle scenes they are counterpointed in the form of musical signals. But the relationship to what is being enacted can also be reflected indirectly, through the prism as it were of the music itself. Thus the Latin church singing (which contrasts

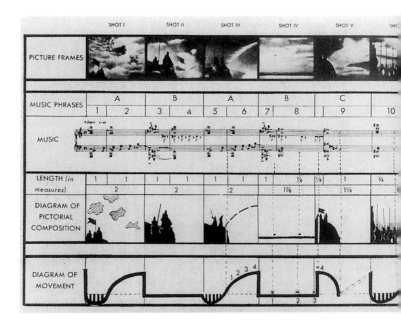

with the Russian folk music) invokes – through citation – the Western world. As a sign of the 'foreign' it becomes a symbol of the threat.[293] And finally Prokofiev's music sometimes also acquires dramatic significance by fore-shadowing events in the film.

Eisenstein, who was fascinated by Prokofiev's music, later tried to provide the interaction between music and picture sequence, a concept he called 'vertical montage', with a theoretical foundation by doing a model analysis of the opening sequences of a central episode in the film (the battle on the ice). Eisenstein's diagrams (below) represent an attempt to demonstrate the exact congruence of music and image seen in relation to movement. Changes in direction in the musical notation correspond to ascending and descending contours in the pictures, but also gradations of brightness, emphasis on picture depth, and even the assumed eye-movements of the audience. The perceived arbitrariness, indeed wilfulness of

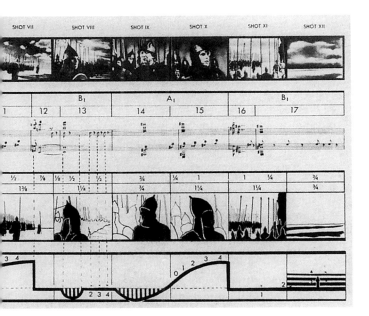

such structural correspondence was criticized in some quarters, but his work had a far reaching impact.[294] Eisenstein's analysis of 1938 reveals a shift in his point of view (informed, no doubt, by the experience of working with a composer like Prokofiev) when set against his concept of contrapuntal montage, laid out in his 1928 *Manifesto on Sound Film*.[295] His vision of a totally integrated film art engendered a new language, the benefits of which can be seen in the work of directors as disparate as Oliver Stone and Steven Spielberg.

Alexander Nevsky was an extraordinary success. Eisenstein and his leading actor, Nikolay Tchekassov, received the Order of Lenin and Prokofiev's contribution received honourable mention. Then with the ebb and flow of German-Soviet relations the film's fortunes fluctuated. Its explicitly anti-German message that 'every person, man, woman or child, should prepare for the possible prospect of war with optimistic feelings',[296] was bound to become embarrassing, indeed a burden, when on 23 August 1939 Stalinist Russia signed its 'non-aggression pact' with Nazi Germany. Naturally, the film's appeal revived after Hitler violated the agreement in 1941. Eisenstein's film was still being shown repeatedly in wartime Vietnam.[297] In the Federal Republic of Germany the work was banned until 1966.

In the summer of 1942 Prokofiev arrived in Alma-Ata. The main United Film Studios of Moscow and Leningrad had been transferred to the Khazak capital. Film had a very special contribution to make in the people's struggle to defend their fatherland. War documentaries presented events as they occurred, and historical feature films reflected the 'eternal greatness' of Russia. Soviet composers wrote film music out of a sense of patriotic duty. Prokofiev regarded this duty rather more soberly: *Film work is interesting and lucrative; and it does not require too much creative energy. Alma-Ata is a pleasant town, and full of money.*[298] Here, as well as writing music for propaganda films, topical stories about Soviet war heroism like Abram Romm's *Tonya*, Fainzimmer's *Kotovski*, Igor Savtchenko's

Partisans in the Ukrainian Steppes, and Albert Gendelstein's film biography *Lermontov,* Prokofiev was also able to resume his collaborative work with Eisenstein.

Eisenstein's film *Ivan the Terrible,* a project capitalizing on the success of *Alexander Nevsky,* that was also politically driven. 'A film about a Titan from the past, Ivan Grosny, and the founding of a unified empire in the 16th-century state of Moscow.'[299] The war lent a fresh topicality to the themes of 'betrayal and conspiracy', and 'unyielding steadfastness in defence of the interests of the empire'.[300] Of course the idealization of the complex and morally ambiguous personality of Ivan the Fourth in terms of a nationalistic world view could not match the runaway success of *Alexander Nevsky,* this would have been a tall order, given the extraordinary degree to which Stalin identified with the Tsar. Eisenstein found a way out of the potential conflict by presenting the ruthless pursuit of power as a guarantee of national unity and independence. The film also reflects Eisenstein's final abandonment of his concept of 'the masses as hero'. The centre of the stage is now dominated by a single sharply delineated character, the figure of an absolute ruler. Broad light-filled outdoor shots show the majesty of the Tsar and field marshals, in sharpest possible contrast to the representatives of feudal fragmentation, the church dignitaries and boyars, dark shadowy figures agitating and conspiring in gloomy cells and crypts. Yet the expressive range of reference of images and music together was extraordinarily wide: *Alternating images of Tsarist palaces, boundless Tartar steppes, sumptuous nuptial banquets, battle fields and snow-bound Russian landscapes appeared upon the screen.*[301] Giving the music many tasks is another dramatically effective feature of Prokofiev the film composer. Thus, the church choir in the coronation scene not only represents itself in its naturalistic function as part of the action being portrayed, but also defines the ambience and location of the scene, the church interior. At a formal level, in its 'even uninterrupted flow' it helps bind together the 'changing content of

Prokofiev and Sergey Eisenstein at the film studios in Alma-Ata in Kazakhstan, collaborating on the score for *Ivan the Terrible*, 1943

the episodes'. Finally, its stylized archaic appearance symbolises the historical remoteness of the images presented.[302]

By the end of 1944 the first part of the film was finished. It was immediately awarded the Stalin prize first class. Eisenstein had planned to extend his original idea into a trilogy of films. A middle part was to have been inserted dealing with the Oprichniki's struggle against the boyars' conspiracy. But as it transpired it was precisely this part, finished in 1946, that Stalin took strong exception to, with the result that it was officially banned until 1958. Stalin objected to what he saw, as Eisenstein's interpretation of the Tsar's historical achievements being merely a personal will to power, that events had been presented in isolation from the struggles of the people, and that a man of 'strong will and character' had been portrayed as 'weak and indecisive, rather in the manner of Hamlet',[303] in fact, as a tragic figure.[304] Eisenstein responded with self-criticism and revisions and after personal discussions with Stalin he managed to get permission to continue his work. Despite this the director was unable to complete the third part. He died in February 1948. The scenes from part three that had already been shot have disappeared.

A still from *Ivan the Terrible.* The Tsar awaits the pleas of the people

It is striking how genres one associates with pure instrumental music continued to crop up among Prokofiev's works during the war years; string quartets, piano sonatas, and symphonies. In the context of threatening events, even a work of chamber music could display national characteristics. Prokofiev's reluctance to make use of material prescribed by others is well known, and his use of authentic folk melodies in his *Second String Quartet* in 1941 should be understood in context. Comparison with the extraordinarily dense *First String Quartet,* written ten years earlier against a more 'academic' background, brings home how 'new' the sound of this later work is. The norms of the traditional genres have now receded. The scoring is less differentiated, the structure of the movements less polyphonal, the tone drier, the sound more compact, the harmonies much more ascerbic. The groundwork of folksong material even legitimizes an overt return to 'Parisian' polytonality. 'It was,' as Myaskovsky remarked, 'simply tremendous, quite awesome in its appeal'.[305] Prokofiev's exemplary synthesis of folk tradition and modern music has affinities with the style of Bartok's string quartets.

With the defeat of the German Sixth Army at Stalingrad in the winter of 1942–43, the war entered a new phase. The cultural institutions were transferred back to the capital, and the artists were free to return too. Ilya Ehrenburg describing the revival of confidence at this period observed that: 'People felt the need to relax and warm up a bit.'[306] One work by Prokofiev in particular has been associated with the mood of these times, the *Flute Sonata in D major.* It was begun in Alma-Ata, and the composer completed it in Perm in the middle of June. He himself described the warmth and lyricism of the sonata *as perhaps not altogether suited to the present point in time, but enjoyable,*[307] and by way of background information mentioned purely musical considerations: the flute as an instrument seemed to him *insufficiently highly regarded in the literature on music.*[308]

The fact that Prokofiev's completion of the triadic *Sixth, Seventh* and *Eighth Piano Sonatas* coincided with the last year of the war has likewise challenged listeners to establish some relationship with external circumstances here too. Sviatoslav Richter felt himself transported by the sonata cycle 'into a world which had lost its balance. Disorder and uncertainty rule. The powers of death and destruction rage before the eyes of people who nevertheless find

The province of Balkar Karbardino lies halfway between the Black and Caspian Seas, in the Northern Caucasus. Prokofiev was among artists exiled to the region as the Nazi invasion of Russia threatened Moscow. Accompanying him was the prodigious Myaskovsky, who had a commission from the regional government to write a *Twenty-Third Symphony* using the striking local folk music. Prokofiev was as thrilled with the beauty of the mountain scenery as he was by the discovery of a rich resource of regional folk music. Goaded by Myaskovsky's prodigious output (he was working on two symphonies and a *Seventh Quartet* while they were in Nalchik), Prokofiev set about an intensive study of the local music. He incorporated the sonority of its instruments, especially the bowed 'lezghinka' into both the sound and structure of the piece; of this, he was inordinately proud. Myaskovsky was almost the only one of Prokofiev's peers who liked the resulting work. By the time Prokofiev had completed the full score of the quartet, in December 1941, the incipient German advance had forced him to move to Tbilisi on the other side of the Caucasian Mountains. When the piece was eventually premièred in Moscow, the following September, he was even further away, in Kazakhstan. This concert was repeatedly interrupted by air raids.

that which makes life worth living continues to survive.'[309] Harsh violence and bold defiance, but sadness and resignation too, are frequently read into these sonatas. They are extraordinarily suggestive in the impact they make, full of harsh dissonances and aggressive sound effects, full of brute strength and unbroken motor-energy, emotionally unbalanced not least in the extreme contrasts set up by the romantic middle movements. But they can be termed 'war sonatas' only with careful qualification. Prokofiev had already begun drafting all ten movements at once by 1939. Moreover, contrary to what one might expect, Prokofiev's specifically patriotic compositions drafted during the war, including the *Fifth Symphony*, tend towards a more lyrical pathos and epic breadth. Prokofiev himself wanted the percussive piano passages, designated as 'con pugno', with the fist, in the score, to be played 'so as to startle grand-mother'.[310] And in fact when he returned to his own instrument, the piano, for the first time since professing himself a Soviet composer, Prokofiev seems to have deliberately taken advantage of the fact that the 'political' parts of these works were relatively uncontroversial so as to indulge in a retrospective reflection on the 'modernist' origins of his piano style. That he was awarded the Stalin prize, in March 1943 expressly for the *Seventh Piano Sonata*, the most complex and radically modern of his sonatas, should perhaps be regarded more as a misunderstanding born out of troubled times, than as a recognition of the aesthetic and compositional merits of this work. After the war the verdict would, all too swiftly, turn to one of harsh criticism.

In October 1943, after an absence of two years, Prokofiev returned to Moscow. He again spent the summer in the 'House of Creativity' run by the Composers' Union near Ivanovo. Here his *Fifth Symphony* took shape. Even more than in the case of the piano sonatas, the reception of this work was determined by circumstance. Shortly before the first performance of the symphony, conducted by the composer himself, news reached the capital that the victorious Red Army had advanced across the River Wisla. It has become common to observe that the symphony reflects and celebrates the impending victory. 'I will never forget the performance of his *Fifth Symphony* in the year 1945, on the eve of the victory,' recalled Sviatoslav Richter. 'It was Prokofiev's last appearance as a conductor . . . He stood on the podium like a monument. And suddenly, as silence descended and he had raised his baton, artillery salvos resounded. He waited and did not begin until the cannons fell silent. What a wealth of symbolic meaning was expressed in this scene. As if a barrier had been lifted in front of everyone.'[311] Even the composer himself frequently alluded to the confessional nature of the symphony, referring to it as an expression of the *'greatness of the human spirit'*,[312] as a *'song to free and happy people'*;[313] or again, reverting to romantic commonplaces of inspiration and inwardness, *I can not say I searched for this theme, it welled up within me and demanded expression. I wrote music that had gradually ripened until it filled my inner being.*[314] The *deeper meaning* of the work Prokofiev located primarily in matters musical and biographical, *not only because of the material dealt with but also on the grounds that with this composition I returned to the symphonic form after a seventeen-year interruption.*[315]

The symphony reaffirmed Prokofiev's prestige and also brought him official Party recognition as the most important and highly regarded composer in the Soviet Union. Prokofiev coveted orders and distinctions and he enjoyed being presented at receptions. But unlike many of his colleagues, Shostakovich included, Prokofiev never received any further honours by accepting official state and Party functions. For him they were merely awards in recognition of his serious and honest work. In 1942 he received a Stalin first prize for the *Seventh Piano Sonata*. Other distinctions included the 'Order of the Red Workers Movement' in 1943, the title 'Working Artist of the Soviet Union' and the 'Order of the Red Army' in 1945. Prokofiev's *Alexander Nevsky* music was performed a record number of times during the war years, both on the screen and as a cantata in concert. The first concert performance of the opera *War and*

Peace, still only with piano accompaniment, was hailed as a musical event. Richter played the piano sonatas repeatedly, the Beethoven quartet, the *Second String Quartet*, and Oistrakh the violin concertos. The composer's fame also grew abroad. Immediately after its first performance, the *Fifth Symphony* was played in Boston and in Paris. In the autumn of 1945 a festival featuring works by Prokofiev was organized. In mid June 1945 he received a gold medal of the 'Royal Philharmonic Society', presented by the British Ambassador in Moscow.

Prokofiev's permanent residency in the Soviet Union, his concessions to the Soviet music industry, and above all the fact that the Soviet bureaucracy was distracted from internal disputes by the real threat posed by Hitler, had all helped to alter his position significantly. At the end of March 1944 there was a plenary meeting of the Organizational Committee in the Composers' Union to discuss developments in Soviet music during the war years. One session was devoted to Prokofiev. Shostakovich gave the introductory lecture: 'His talent has blossomed . . . so wonderfully in our time . . . his influence on many composers is very significant indeed.'[316]

Shortly after the first performance of the *Fifth Symphony*, a fall left Prokofiev with a severe concussion that was to be the beginning of a long period of illness. He was never to recover completely.

Zhdanovshtchina [317]

The collapse of both Prokofiev's personal and his political fortunes after 1945 may or may not have been a coincidence. But in any event, the common assertion in much writing on Prokofiev, that by the time of his illness and the Party criticisms of 1948, his best years as a composer were over, certainly warrants reconsideration.

During the first years after the war Prokofiev enjoyed increasing recognition as a Soviet composer. His pre-eminent standing was confirmed by the many first performances and prizes. In the space of just one year, between November 1945 and December 1946, five of his works appeared in new productions on the stage in Moscow and Leningrad. On 21 November 1945 the long awaited première of *Cinderella*, choreographed by Rostislav Sacharov, was held at the Bolshoi Theatre. Its positive reception was reflected in a review in *Pravda*, in which Shostakovich placed the work 'in the shining tradition of Russian ballet'.[318] In the spring of 1946 the Kirov Theatre in Leningrad included Prokofiev's music in its repertoire to its own new choreography. After the success of the complete concert performance of *War and Peace* in June 1945 with the Moscow State Symphony Orchestra, Samosud, who had meanwhile become artistic director of the Maly Theatre in Leningrad, was able to plan a full-scale production of the monumental work. On 12 June, Samuel Samosud conducted the stage première of the first part of the opera in a production by Boris Pokrovsky. By March 1947 fifty performances had been given, an unusual success for a new opera, especially a work as demanding as this. The second part was expected to run during the coming season. The success of the Leningrad première of the comic opera *Betrothal in a Monastery* at the Kirov Theatre in November 1946 was likewise reflected in enthusiastic reviews. Shostakovich even risked a comparison with Verdi's *Falstaff*.[319] Finally in December the first Bolshoi production of the ballet *Romeo and Juliet* (this would gain world renown, encouraged by the wide release of a filmed version) completed these triumphs.

In 1947, the thirtieth anniversary of the Revolution, Prokofiev was awarded the honorary title of 'People's Artist of the Soviet Union'. His main compositions for that year were connected with the jubilee celebrations, the commemorative poem *The Year 1941* (*Thirty Years*), the cantata *Flourish, O Mighty Land*, and the *Sixth Symphony*. Prokofiev's oratorical work is infused with patriotic sentiment throughout.

Thus there is an extra-musical dimension at the heart of these musical configurations, a textual core with functional objectives. It is precisely this dimension that has often attracted the censure of Western critics, who have complained of a loss of musical quality in the pursuit of political affirmatives. In these works the composer was looking for a simple accessible musical idiom in these works. The curtailment of more innovative musical devices in the interests of illustrating the text is manifest. It is characteristic of Prokofiev that even in such official works he was not prepared to relinquish the wider imperatives of Art. None of his compositions could ever be held up as a representative model of state music. Even the *Ode to the End of the War*, Prokofiev's contribution to the peace celebrations of 1946, did not meet with unqualified approval. Indeed, it is not a particularly 'accessible' work, but raw and eccentric, dense-sounding and rather austerely structured. Moreover, its prodigal instrumentation (the orchestration demands expanded brass and percussion sections, four pianos, and eight harps) made scarcely practicable demands.

Since 1947 Prokofiev had spent the greater part of the year in his dacha in Nikolina Gora. Here, thanks to the inheritance of a house, the 'world citizen' finally found a permanent home. In the neighbourhood of close friends and shielded from the political upheavals in the capital, he was able to devote himself uninterrupted to composition: work on the second part of *Ivan the Terrible*, completion of scores for the Moscow staging of *Romeo and Juliet*, plans for a new scene in the second part of *War and Peace*, the orchestration of the *Sixth Symphony*, and drafts of the *Cello Sonata*, the *Cinderella* suites and the 'Waltz' *Symphonic Suite* (waltzes adapted from *Cinderella*, *War and Peace*, and the music for the film *Lermontov*).

Another high point of Prokofiev's career as a Soviet composer was receiving a series of Stalin prizes in recognition of his long

David Oistrakh (1908–1974) was the most important Soviet violinist. He was born in Odessa, in the Ukraine, where he studied with the great pedagogue Stoliarsky, and had a lifelong association with living composers, which began when he played Glazunov's concerto under the baton of the composer at the age of fourteen. Shostakovich, Kabalevsky, Khachaturian, Myaskovsky, and Prokofiev all dedicated works to Oistrakh, whose interpretations of their works has been regarded as a benchmark ever since. He played and recorded all of Prokofiev's violin music, the two concerti, the *Cinq Melodies* and the innovatory *Sonata for Two Violins*, which he played many times with his son, the virtuoso Igor Oistrakh. In 1944, Oistrakh helped Prokofiev to make a violin transcription of his *Flute Sonata*, and it became equally successful in this version. In 1947 Prokofiev dedicated his highly evocative *F minor Sonata* Op 80 to Oistrakh. Oistrakh was Prokofiev's equal as a chess player, and in 1937 the two played a public contest in Moscow. The loser had to play a concert, whilst the winner was allowed to join the audience. Oistrakh won. It has to be said that Oistrakh was prone to over-emphasizing his relationship to Prokofiev's violin music, and many commentators fall into the trap of not recognizing the importance of Prokofiev's earlier, and far more innovatory, collaborations with Paul Kochanski, Josef Szigeti, and Albert Spalding, all of whom were greater innovators on the instrument than Oistrakh, whose technical and musical approach was essentially conservative. The volcanic early recordings of his son Igor, particularly of the *First Violin Concerto*, are perhaps much closer to the acerbic spirit of the young Prokofiev when he wrote this radical piece.

years of service. The works singled out for distinction – with first class prizes – in January 1946 were the *Fifth Symphony*, the *Eighth Piano Sonata* and also the first part of *Ivan the Terrible*. A prize for *Cinderella* followed in July. During the summer of 1947 Prokofiev had also managed, after eight years, to complete his *First Violin Sonata*. Even this work, expressively stretched to the limit, dramatically intense, linking it with the *First String Quartet* and like that work harking back to late Beethoven, was awarded a Stalin prize. A caricature which appeared in con-

David Oistrakh

junction with the protracted celebrations for Prokofiev's fifty-fifth birthday shows the artist crowned with laurels but bowed down by the weight of further new scores.

With its victory in the Great Patriotic War and its rise to the status of a world power, the Soviet Union had become the focus of much interest in the West, especially in the United States. There Soviet art and culture – in those days little known – became something of a fad. Soviet composers were frequently brought over and repeatedly received mention in the press. Prokofiev's *Fifth Symphony* had its American première in Boston under Koussevitzky. The composer received greetings and invitations from all over America. In the Soviet Union, of course, the end of the war also meant the end of a brief period of relaxation in relations between art and politics. But the hopes that had been raised, abroad as well as in Russia, by Stalin's victory, were not to be fulfilled. Under the banner of reconstruction, the dictator reinstated rigid ideological discipline as his first priority. The consequences were strict external boundary demarcations and increased pressure to conform internally. The

FIRST VIOLIN SONATA

Andrey Zhdanov, Cultural Commissar and scourge of Russian artists

new tone was set in a speech by Stalin in February 1946. The mood of victorious self-assurance had given way to warnings of the need for vigilance. The new man in charge during the latest upheavals was Andrey Zhdanov. During the war Zhdanov had been Party secretary in Leningrad, and since 1945 he had become head of the Central Committee's propaganda section. Zhdanov died in 1948, but this did not have any effect on 'Zhdanovshtchina' policies at all: Soviet culture remained rigidly regimented until Stalin's death – and well beyond it.

On 14 August 1946, an official resolution of the Cultural Committee found the literary journals *Sveda* (*Star*) and *Leningrad* guilty of publishing 'ideologically harmful' works. Those specifically targeted were the lyric poet Anna Akhmatova and the satirist Mikhail Zoshchenko.[320] In two speeches at the Writers' Congress in September 1946, Zhdanov voiced his criticisms in personally insulting terms. And his advance raid gave the signal for an extension of the campaign – first of all to theatre and film. However, Zhdanov's resolutions, especially his fight against 'cosmopolitanism' and 'Western decadence', were by no means unpopular. They appealed to the Soviet patriotism of the war years, which now in the guise of post-war nationalism resumed its earlier anti-Western sentiment with renewed zeal.[321] In the winter of 1947/48 music finally came under attack. The political line was not fundamentally new, but its radical implementation was. Over and above the mere banning of certain musical works, concrete guidelines for composition were laid down. In music, the resolutions meant far more than merely the hardening of long-familiar positions. With the discrediting of idols that the Party and the government press themselves had built up over the years, the discussion acquired a new dimension. Prokofiev, Shostakovich, Myaskovsky, and Khachaturian were officially protected as composers through their state commissions, their prizes, and the laudatory criticism of the Party press. Even during the attacks on the adjacent disciplines, Prokofiev had managed to chalk up several successes, in fact his greatest as a Soviet composer. But Zhdanov's tribunal of January 1948, as decisive as it was unannounced, brought this series of triumphs to an end.

One warning sign, similar to Shostakovich's *Lady Macbeth of the Mtsensk District* in 1936, though not made as spectacularly public, was the cancellation of the second part of *War and Peace* at the Maly Theatre in Leningrad in July 1947. The opera had been shown in a closed performance to a panel of musical and cultural-cum-political authorities and had received an entirely positive response. But a little later the picture changed. 'Errors' had been discovered in the historical conceptualization of the military scenes. Yet if the artistic coherence of the whole were to be maintained, Prokofiev could not possibly make the scene cuts that were being demanded. After further closed performances the second part of the opera was banned from public performance. It was not until 1957 that the opera was finally staged in thirteen scenes on a single evening.

Likewise, restrictions were imposed on the Moscow première of Prokofiev's *Sixth Symphony*, which had been so warmly received in Leningrad. The drafts of the work go back to the period of the celebrated *Fifth Symphony*, and this proximity in time is matched by corresponding affinities in style. *In composing it I was trying to reproduce in music my admiration for the power of the human spirit as it has manifested itself so brilliantly in our time and in our country.*[322] One of the distinguishing features of the *Sixth Symphony*, which as Op 111 is appropriately dedicated to the memory of Beethoven, is its compliance with socialist-realist principles. Its primal simplicity, clear formal conceptualization, unified structuring of block-like sequences, and crystal-clear orchestration all live up to the criteria demanded for broad popular appeal. The underlying tone is narrative, controlled by broad diatonic melodies, whose grandiose theatricality, particularly in the long middle movement, reflects a reversion to various thematic prototypes in Prokofiev's Soviet opera, ballet, and film music. In the closing third movement, the powerful harmonious forward surge of the music expresses the optimism one associates with the dramatic strategy so often adopted by the traditional symphony, 'Through the night into the light'.

In the programme notes for the Moscow première, the Soviet critic Grigory Schneyerson still felt free to commend Prokofiev's symphony as 'one of the most beautiful and uplifting of his works, full of the creative spirit of Soviet humanism'.[323] Now the critics reproached the composer for his deliberate and artificial complexity. The symphony vanished from the repertoire of Soviet orchestras for many years. The score was first published by a New York publishing house.

Then the official pretext for the 'musical upheavals in Moscow'[324] was given by the première of the opera *The Great Friendship* by the Georgian composer Vano Muradeli. First, quite out of the blue, no more works by contemporary composers appeared on the programmes, then Sviatoslav Richter, in a concert where he was to play Prokofiev's *Ninth Piano Sonata*, played Schubert instead, without any explanation. In the middle of January 1948, a three-day scholarly convention of the Composers' Union disclosed the Party's dissatisfaction with the state of operatic writing.[325] Then, an official resolution of the Party's Central Committee on 10 February denounced Muradeli's opera, both music and libretto.[326] Referring explicitly to the criticism of Shostakovich in *Pravda* in 1936, and to the recently enacted resolutions on literature, theatre, and film, the critical assault now widened: 'Heedless of these warnings and contrary to these directives . . . no changes have been introduced in Soviet music. The individual success of some composers in creating new songs which have achieved recognition by the people and been

John Minnion's caricature of Prokofiev and Shostakovich, among the most prominent victims of post-war Soviet censure

widely disseminated, cannot alter the general picture of the situation in the area of film composition. The situation is particularly bad with regard to symphonic and operatic composition. There we are dealing with composers who continue to subscribe to formalist tendencies which are alien to the people. These tendencies have found their strongest expression in the works of composers like Shostakovich, Prokofiev, Khachaturian, Popov, Myaskovsky and others.'[327]

In the press, Soviet musicians were immediately reported as being in enthusiastic agreement with the resolutions.[328] A special meeting of the Composers' Union was convened. Zhdanov took control of the opening proceedings.[329] Tikhon Khrennikov, the new Secretary General of the Union (who managed to stay afloat in that position through all subsequent political changes, even beyond the collapse of the Soviet Union) spelled out the party guidelines in a lengthy historical appeal.[330] Socialist realism was defined no longer as a purely aesthetic concept but as a political programme, as an ideological stance. These events reverberated internationally. The ensuing discussions at the 'Second International Congress of

Tikhon Khrennikov, Secretary General of the Composers' Union

Composers and Music Critics' in Prague in May (Khrennikov was also a member of the Soviet delegation), and the discarding of the so called 'Prague Manifesto'[331] challenged Western cultural leaders to commit themselves and take up a position. Hanns Eisler[332] was in favour of agreeing with the Soviet line. Adorno[333] and Sartre[334] expressed their reservations. Among the comments that have retained more permanent relevance are René Leibowitz's[335] reflections on the possibilities for an integration of art and socio-political engagement. In the long run, Leibowitz's ideas would have the biggest impact, particularly on the politicized works of his greatest pupil, Hans Werner Henze.[336]

Prokofiev had been absent from the January meeting of the Soviet Composers' Union on the grounds of ill health. Once more, he was reprimanded for his Western roots, for the connection of his music with the 'decadent, pathological and perverted'[337] foreign music scene. In a letter to Khrennikov and Polikarp Lebedev, the chairman of the Committee for Cultural Affairs, he defended himself against the accusations. What he wrote is certainly not a document of self-righteous defiance. The composer did not question the Party's right to criticize. Yet the factual nature of his argument avoids comparable self-renunciations and submissive statements to the Party made by other artists. Prokofiev responded only to the musical implications of the resolution, without getting involved in the main ideological debate:

Elements of Formalism were still present in my music some fifteen to twenty years ago. I was probably infected by contact with a whole series of Western influences. Since the exposure of the formalist errors in Shostakovich's opera through 'Pravda' on the instructions of the Central Committee of the

Communist Party of the Soviet Union, I have reflected a great deal on the stylistic devices in my music, and have come to recognize the erroneousness of such a path. There then followed a search for a clearer and inherently more substantive language. In a series of my works, for instance 'Alexander Nevsky', 'Toast to Stalin', 'Romeo and Juliet' or in the 'Fifth Symphony,' I have tried to free myself from these elements of Formalism, and to me at least it seems that to a certain extent I have succeeded . . .

On the question of the significance of melody, for me there was never any doubt. I love melody very much, consider it one of the most important elements in music and for years have been working to improve its quality in my works. The hardest thing for a composer is to find a melody which is both immediately understandable to the uninitiated listener and at the same time original. In doing so innumerable dangers lie in wait for him: lapsing into what is trivial or banal or repeating what has already been achieved. In this respect composing more complicated melodies is significantly easier. It can happen that the composer who labours at length over his melody and repeatedly corrects it, himself does not notice that in the process it becomes artificial and complicated and loses its simplicity. In the course of my work I have doubtless fallen into this trap. When composing one must proceed with special care, so that the melody remains simple and yet not cheap, imitative or saccharine. That is easy to say but all the harder to put into practice, and all my efforts will go into ensuring that these words do not remain empty precepts but will be realized in my future works . . .

I have often been reproached for the fact that in my operas the recitative predominates over the cantilena. I love the stage as such and believe that a person who has come to an opera house has the right to demand not only impressions for the ear but also impressions for the eye (otherwise he would not have gone to the opera but to a concert). Yet every movement on stage is more linked to the recitative, whereas the cantilena carries with it a measure of immobility . . . The allusion in the Central Committee's Resolution to the desirability of polyphony, especially in choral and ensemble singing, gave me great pleasure. That is indeed an interesting task for the composer and a great pleasure to the listener . . .

In conclusion, I should like to express my gratitude to the Party for the clear guidelines in the Resolution, which are of help to me in my search for a comprehensible musical language intimately connected with the people, which is worthy of our people and our great country.[338]

For fourteen years Prokofiev had laboured under the conviction that he, more than anyone else, represented the musical language of his people. This belief had enabled him to remain true to his compositional objectives, and the numerous accolades he had received seemed to strengthen his mandate as the 'people's artist'. Now he realized that neither his international reputation, nor his longstanding popularity with the public and the press within the Soviet Union could protect him from attack by the Party.

While the February conference was still in session Prokofiev received another blow. Lina Prokofiev was arrested. Stalin's attitude to writers and artists was rigorous and uncompromising. They were threatened under the 'Zhdanovshtchina' with opprobrium and humiliation, though no longer with arrest and death. The deportation and murder of many creative people in the arts (one need only remember Meyerhold, Osip Mandelstam, and Pavel Florenski), during the reign of terror in the 1930s spoke a harsher language. In general Stalin now handled artists differently from political and military suspects. Unarguably, Prokofiev's wife Lina was a political case.

Since 1941 Prokofiev had been living with Mira Mendelson, a young poet and librettist he had got to know in Kislovodsk a few summers earlier. The circumstances of their marriage in 1948 were for a long time unclear. Lina Prokofiev never consented to a divorce. As a 'foreigner', although in possession of a Soviet passport, she was fearful for her safety in the increasingly xenophobic atmosphere of Stalinist Russia, justifiably so as it turned out. Her connection with the Soviet composers who were also most prominent abroad protected her. Prokofiev's remarriage was finally made possible by the new marriage laws of 1944: Sergey and Lina

Prokofiev's marriage, formalized abroad and not resumed after 1944, was no longer legally valid.[339]

For Lina Prokofiev the composer's decision to remarry threatened her entire existence. It is hardly conceivable that he was not aware of the danger to his wife. On the other hand, given the puritanical bourgeois morality of Stalinist society, he could no longer avoid legalizing his relationship with Mira Mendelson. Being hard-pressed as an artist, Prokofiev thought this was the time to set his personal affairs in order, at least in this regard.

Lina Prokofiev was Spanish by birth, and her marriage had taken place in Germany. She was in touch with friends and relatives in Europe and America. She was a regular guest at the American embassy, and she had put in an application to travel abroad. All of this was more than enough for her to be accused of spying. On 20 February 1948 Lina Prokofiev was abducted from her apartment under false pretences, imprisoned and eventually charged with passing information to foreign persons. She was sentenced to twenty years of hard labour. After eight years in a camp in Siberia she was finally able to return to Moscow in 1956. In 1974 Lina Prokofiev left the Soviet Union, moving through Paris, New York and London. She died in 1989 in London at the age of ninety-one. Until the very end she insisted that her marriage was still valid, and until the end she devoted herself to promoting her husband's work. 'His life was my life too. What came afterwards is not important.'[340]

Prokofiev has often been blamed for not having exerted himself courageously enough in his wife's defence. By all accounts, Prokofiev did try to help, drafting petitions and applications for her release. The timing of Lina's arrest was evidently carefully considered. Prokofiev's reputation as an artist had been severely damaged, he was ill, and accusations of contact with the West had also been levelled against him. Lina Prokofiev's arrest was a powerful demonstration of the Party's control over the composer. There is no other interpretation possible. The existential angst and spiritual crippling

Prokofiev experienced indicate how fully he realized this himself.

Since the 1920s Prokofiev had been trying out new musical and dramatic possibilities for opera. One idea that seemed promising was for an exemplary 'Soviet' opera, a national confessional work presented in the officially approved idiom and taste. But revival of *Khan-Busay*, a lyrical comic opera based on a Khazak folk saga, which Prokofiev had begun in Alma-Ata as early as 1942, did not quite seem to fit the bill.[341] On this occasion material that might be suited to the times could not afford to be historically remote. Boris Polevoy's novel *The Story of a True Man* met Prokofiev's requirements: *I dedicate my new opera to the Soviet citizen and to his boundless courage.*[342] The fateful Resolution of the Central Committee of 10 February 1948 seemed to endorse the composer's plans. The subject matter was in complete conformity with the principles of 'socialist realism.' It depicts the heroic deeds of a Soviet world war pilot, Alexey Maresyev,[343] a hero of the Second World War and an exemplary member of society. Prokofiev's music fulfils every conceivable party requirement as regards clarity, accessibility and understandability. The fact that it was precisely this opera that should be rejected following a closed concert performance, the objections being translated into the usual jargon of 'formalist', 'modernist', 'antimelodic', and 'lacking in true understanding of Soviet heroism',[344] must have been particularly depressing for the composer. It certainly shows how little recognition depended on intrinsically artistic criteria. Prokofiev's apologetic letter to the Presidency of the Composers' Union on 28 December 1948 should be seen as a despairing attempt to rescue his work for performance: *I have tried to be as melodic as possible in my opera and to make the melodies as understandable as possible. My first concern in the portrait of the hero was to reveal the inner life of a Soviet citizen – his love of our country, his Soviet patriotism.*[345] It was a forlorn hope. The opera was not staged until 1960, though it was then quickly and widely disseminated throughout the socialist-bloc countries. But for many years Prokofiev's music vanished almost

Formalism in Soviet and communist terms, is a pejorative deriving from the group of literary analysts working in Russia before the 1917 revolution. Led by Viktor Shlovsky, and including the leading constructivist theoritician Boris Arvatov, it studied the stylistic features and formal structure of literary and artistic works. Its influence can be seen, as a positive force, in the analytical methods and structural tropes of the works of Eisenstein. With the rise of the socialist realist doctrine, from 1934 onwards, the term was expanded to include any perceived over-preoccupation with the formal and architectural conceits of art, as opposed to content, and was thus condemned as heretical and anti-populist and lacking in social commitment. The term became an all-embracing weapon with which all of the recent abstract schools of art could be attacked. The implication was that there was a direct correlation between the individual vanity or intellectual exclusivity, and Western capitalism. Abstract art and 'twelve-tone music' were its particular targets; one result was that the impact of the 'Second Viennese School' of composers was not felt in Russia until Hershkowitz and Denisov started teaching the serial theory in Moscow in the late 1960s.

totally from the musical life of the Soviet Union.

The *Ninth Piano Sonata* in C Major is Prokofiev's last completed work for piano, dedicated to Sviatoslav Richter, the leading interpreter of his piano music. *The Sonata for Solo Violin* is a pedagogical work for violin students, it was intended for group performance with an ensemble of twenty violinists. The language of the sonata is an interesting return to the 'sprung', simple rhythms and harmonic simplicity of the *Classical Symphony*, particularly in the march-like opening movement. In the years after Prokofiev's death, the sonata won a large following as a work for one player, particularly in the West, where the Soviet tradition of unison violin 'choirs' (such as the Violins of the Bolshoi Theatre) never took hold.

Prokofiev's collaboration with the cellist Mstislav Rostropovitch was also particularly productive. In 1947 Rostropovitch had retrieved Prokofiev's *First Cello Concerto* from oblivion, and in the spring of 1949 Prokofiev composed the *Sonata for Cello and Piano* for him.

The *Sonata* is a beautiful example of his late style, simple in

Sviatoslav Richter (1915–) Was brought up in Odessa, and studied under Neuhaus in Moscow. He was awarded the Stalin prize in 1949. Prokofiev dedicated his three war-time sonatas to him. He came to international attention after playing with the Philadelphia Orchestra on its 1958 tour of the Soviet Union. The work he played with them was Prokofiev's *Fifth Concerto*, and thereafter his powerful and highly polished pianism was closely associated with Prokofiev. He was also closely associated with the music of Shostakovich, and premièred his *Violin Sonata* at David Oistrakh's sixtieth birthday concert. Benjamin Britten dedicated his *Piano Concerto* to him.

harmony and rhythm, with sustained soft warm cello passages sparely accompanied on the piano, and full of light-heartedness and humour, though not free from gallows humour. The reworking of the originally quite unsuccessful *Cello Concerto* into the *Symphonic Concerto for Cello and Orchestra*, with its exploitation of 'all the resources of the instrument both technical and expressive',[346] again reflects Prokofiev's close collaboration with Rostropovich. But the new title also announces an enhancement of the orchestra's role. In the finale one can clearly perceive the effect of Party resolutions of 1948 and the composer's self-critical response. This is evident in the reorientation of the content: the 'emphasis on the lyrical element' in the 'quest for a contemplative and clarified mode of expression';[347] the formal restructuring of the movement from a rhapsodic freely developed sequence of variations into a clearly articulated three-part structure; and especially the integration of

Prokofiev and Rostropovich outside the Moscow Conservatory, 1950

folksong elements into the middle section of the movement.[348]

With Prokofiev's last ballet, *The Stone Flower*, the use of a fairy-tale, plus its intimate connection with folklore, to some degree stylistically legitimizes the music's retrospective stance; similarly, in his new pieces for and about children, Prokofiev managed to attain the

Mstislav Rostropovich (1927–). Along with the Catalan Cellist Pablo Casals, Mstislav Rostropovich can lay claim to being one of the greatest all-round musicians and consciences of the 20th century. He was born by the Caspian Sea in Baku, in 1927; his father was a cellist, and had been a student of Casals. His mother taught at the Gnesin Institute, so a musical career was inevitable; in 1947 he went to the Moscow Conservatory to study composition with Shostakovich and Shebalin. After winning a number of prestigious competitions, he was awarded the Stalin prize in 1951. In 1956, he was made a full cello professor at the Moscow Conservatory, where amongst his students, he numbered the young Jacqueline du Pré. From the very beginning he has remained totally committed to the work of living composers, whilst being renowned for his benchmark performances of the great concerti, most particularly his peerless account of the Dvorak Concerto.

After considerable work with the composer, Rostropovich gave the world première of Prokofiev's *Sinfonia Concertante* in 1952. From then on, Rostropovich was responsible for a stream of premières that continues unabated to this day, winning acclaim as cellist, opera conductor and as pianist for his wife, the great soprano, Galina Vishnevskaya. In recent years he has championed the concerti of British resident composers, from the émigré Pole Andrezj Panufnik, to David Matthews and James Macmillan. As conductor of the National Symphony Orchestra in Washington, he conducted premières of work from established masters such as Henri Dutilleux through to young Americans such as August Read Thomas. But it will not be for all of this that he will be primarily remembered, but rather for his refusal to bow to Soviet officialdom, and for his support for neglected and oppressed Russian artists and thinkers.

officially prescribed simplicity and optimism in the lyrical flow of the melodies. His *Winter Camp Fire* suite for narrator, boys' choir, and orchestra has affinities with the fairy story *Peter and the Wolf*. In eight programmatic movements the work depicts a group of young pioneers walking through the woods in winter, within the framework of a musically illustrated railway journey. Here too a narrative text links the musical sections and the instruments are allotted appropriate functions. But Prokofiev had a higher opinion of his comprehensive ten-movement oratorio *On Guard for Peace*. What is especially interesting about this work is the presentation of the theme of peace in scenes from the lives of children. *I did not go looking for this theme, nor did I choose it. It grew on me out of life itself, from life's bustle, from everything that surrounds and moves us, myself and other people . . . In this work I wanted to express my thoughts on peace and war, as well as my conviction that there will be no more war, that the peoples of the earth will defend peace, in order to save and to preserve civilization, our children and our future.*[349]

The first performance of these works in December 1950 was hailed as an important event in Soviet musical life, while also contributing to the rehabilitation of the composer. For the first time since the fateful Resolution, Prokofiev was again in the public eye. The following year both works were awarded a Stalin prize second class.

The Meeting of the Volga and Don is an official work composed to a celebratory ode written to commemorate the opening of the canal link between the Volga and Don in 1951. The composer described this work in the inflated rhetoric of Stalinist publicity, emphasizing appropriate catchwords like country, people, tradition, singability, and optimism: *As I worked I thought about the wide unending world of our two great rivers, listened in spirit to the songs about them that have arisen among the people, and to the verses our classic and contemporary poets have dedicated to them. I have tried to make the music to the poems singable and a true reflection of the delight in creativity our entire people today is seized by.*[350] Musically, however, the piece operates at a high level with a rich compositional palette – lyricism, drama, colouring, and wit.

In 1949 Boris Asafyev died in 1950, after forty-five years of friendship, Nikolay Myaskovsky; in 1951 Prokofiev lost Pavel Lamm, the last of his group of close friends. Prokofiev himself was so ill that he could not even attend Myaskovsky's funeral. It was as though his life were being taken from him piece by piece. After weeks in hospitals and sanatoria, he spent the summer of 1951 in Nikolina Gora under strict instructions from his doctors not to compose. In April 1951, on the occasion of Prokofiev's sixtieth birthday, the

Composers' Union celebrated him as the most significant composer of the Soviet Union. On 11 October 1952 the composer appeared in public for the last time at a concert in his honour, which included the first successful performance of his *Seventh Symphony*. In 1953 he was obliged to turn down an invitation to Brussels as a jury member in the 'Queen Elisabeth of the Belgians' Composers' Competition on the grounds of ill health. He spent the winter in Moscow on doctors' orders. In February his strength declined further. On 1 March rehearsals for the ballet *The Stone Flower* began at Moscow's Bolshoi Theatre. On the evening of 5 March 1953, at almost the same hour as Joseph Stalin,[351] Sergey Prokofiev died.

I could, I should have composed so much more.[352] Prokofiev's last completed work was the *Seventh Symphony* in C sharp minor. Laid out in four movements, the symphony begins with a song-like sonata movement (moderato), followed by an elegiac waltz (allegretto) and a lyrical andante espressivo, rounded out with a lively dance finale (vivace). There is clear evidence that in this work the composer tried to work strictly within the constraints of the Stalinist musical ideal, in the directness of musical expression and the optimism of the underlying tone, in the clarity of structure, the diatonic harmony of contour and the transparency of its orchestration, in the strictly functional tonality and the flowing melodic lyricism, and in the assimilation of folk music elements into the thematic concepts. Even *Pravda* could extol Prokofiev's renunciation of the 'baroque excrescences' of Formalism and his dedication to the aesthetic requirements of the Soviet people. Shostakovich praised the work as 'one of the purest compositions of our era'.[353] The idea of 'youth' has also been seen as the programmatic theme of the symphony.[354] In 1957, before the Party Congress of 1958 had officially declared Zhdanov's Resolutions to have been an 'error', Prokofiev's *Seventh Symphony* was posthumously awarded what after Stalin's death became known as the Lenin prize.

In the West the work was controversial. On the one hand the

The last photograph of Prokofiev taken at Nikolina Gora in the Autumn of 1952

circumstances of its composition, the political pressures and the illness of the composer together invited the censure of its more uncomplicated aspects as a total 'lapse into banality'.[355] Such criticism found Prokofiev's last composition 'hollow' and 'lamentably thread-bare':[356] 'The work cannot be regarded as a serious or ground-breaking expression of his symphonic thinking.'[357] At most, adopting more neutral evaluative criteria, critics were prepared to attribute 'naïvety' to the composer in this work.[358] On the other hand the artlessness of Prokofiev's tribute to the dictates of official cultural doctrine was bound to rouse suspicions. The plasticity of the lyric phrases seemed at times to border all too obviously on the banal for the composer to be credited with consistently serious intentions. Might not mockery, satire, irony, and scorn have, once again, been guiding his pen? Once before, in the classicizing inventiveness of his *First Symphony*, the composer had been prompted by a *declared intention of annoying the philistines*.[359] How much more must he now have been disposed to hoist state cultural philistinism by the petard of its own prejudices. Was it a case of sublime rebellion, or simply resignation? Put thus, the question is misleading. The symphony has seldom been dispassionately evaluated in terms of its compositional decorum, purposeful abstractness, and strict simplicity. Edward Lockspeiser for example disappointedly asserts that the work does not reflect 'the final triumph of seriousness one might have expected such a composer to have reached'.[360]

What about the absence of conflict as a symphonic idea? Here one can find a bridge back to Prokofiev's so unreservedly successful first symphonic work. Both symphonies tackle a self-appointed task within the constraints of particular restrictions. In the *Classical Symphony* the composer sets himself the task of *for once composing an entire symphonic work without the aid of the piano*.[361] Now it was a question of exploiting the possibilities of symphonic within the rigid guidelines imposed by socialist realism.

The extent to which the expectations of the Composers' Union played a part in Prokofiev's composing is revealed by an incident recalled by Dmitri Kabalevsky: 'One of my memorable visits to Prokofiev in Nikolina Gora is connected in my mind with his then recently completed *Seventh Symphony*. At the time he was unable to make the trip into Moscow, and he had agreed to a performance of his new work in the Composers' Union without his being present. A piano adaptation of the symphony was superbly played by Alexander Vedernikov and received with general applause. As we knew how anxious Prokofiev was about the fate of his new work, I went out . . . to Nikolina Gora the next day. Sergey Sergeyevich was feeling ill and lay in bed. Eagerly he asked about the impression the symphony had made. And how joyfully he smiled, how immediately he perked up as soon as he heard it was a success. Fearing lest what we had said might be prompted by our desire to keep his strength and spirits up, he kept asking further questions. 'Is not the music perhaps too simple?' he wanted to know suddenly.'[362]

The work is not a parody, not a joke. But it is also not part of a personal confession. It is the presentation of a symphonic idea within special compositional constraints. Prokofiev's compositional departure from the stage of life was a prudent one. But with him prudence never meant loss of personality. The unmediated, the here and now, are part and parcel of his being. They are also part and parcel of his style of music.

Epilogue

The conflicts and contradictions of the days around Prokofiev's death and funeral are oddly germane to the issues that affected his life and, to a degree, still prevent a balanced consideration of his oeuvre.

Within an hour of Prokofiev's death, his great goad and nemesis, Joseph Stalin, was dead.

In his cantata, *Zdravitsa* (*Toast to Stalin*) (1939), Prokofiev had set the following lines:

> 'If my eyes sparkled as when I was a girl.
> If my cheeks were as red as an apple ripe,
> I would hie me to Moscow, the great city
> And say, "Thank you" to Joseph Stalin.'

The solemn announcements of the long anticipated and oft-rumoured death of Stalin on Soviet Radio were greeted with extraordinary scenes across the Russias. In the labour camps and prison yards of the Gulag Archipelago, the reverent tones of the specially selected announcers (only the most famous broadcasters were deemed to carry sufficient gravitas and class – for 'Uncle Joe' was a snob) were in stark contrast to the wild exultation of the over-excited prison populations, who were jumping for joy, not only the death of their tormentor, but in the expectation of their imminent release.[363] This was, in most cases, a chimera. It was rumoured that every drop of wine and liquor to be had on the day of Stalin's demise was drunk in an orgy of celebration and grief. If the whole of the Soviet Union was united on one thing, it was in the emotional outpouring which followed his death. One wonders how the news was greeted by Prokofiev's first and possibly only wife, who would be behind bars until 1957, or the pianist Topllin, who had been Oistrakh's duo partner in the early days when he was trailblazing towards international superstardom, who was also languishing in a labour camp.[364] One thing is for sure, neither they nor most of the country would hear a word of Prokofiev's death for some time to come; his death was first reported internationally, and did not reach the Moscow papers until 11 March.

March 5 had begun, for Prokofiev, in a mood of some irritation, and the prospect of a day of compositional labour, under pressure, lay ahead of him. Naturally enough, he was pleased with the news which Lavrovsky had given him at his dacha at Nikolina Gora a few weeks before, that the Bolshoi Theatre was about to put *The Stone Flower* into production, and that he was starting rehearsals.[365] Prokofiev was placed under a strict regimen, after his illnesses of the past years, by his doctor, Elena Teppler; she ordered him to seriously restrict the stressful hours of composing which he allowed himself. But he now disregarded her advice, and set to work with a vengeance, despite his influenza.[366] Over recent years, an irrational tendency had emerged, a barely hidden conviction that he could stave off death by work. He probably didn't have much choice, as he was under considerable pressure to make an escalating number of changes to his ballet score, and working to a very tight deadline, with rehearsals hard on the heels of his completed revisions. This would be stressful enough for a young and energetic man, but for a composer recently recovered from serious illness, and now in the grip of influenza, it was potentially fatal. Actual rehearsals for the ballet began on 1 March, and Prokofiev's high spirits carried him forward.[367] In point of fact, Prokofiev's very last composition, his revision of the *pas de deux*, the adagio from *The Stone Flower*, actually dates from the day of his death, 5 March.[368] Prokofiev's happiness at the impending production of *The Stone Flower*, was tempered to some degree by his anger at discovering that his score was not considered to be perfect by the Bolshoi. Leonid Lavrovsky brought him repeated demands for a variety of structural and textural changes from the company. Old, loaded criticisms of his over-personal orchestration re-emerged – the ghost of the old accusation of 'formalism' which, perhaps, he had hoped had been laid to rest with the optimistic simplicity of the *Seventh Symphony*. The theatre insisted that he 'tone down' his ripe instrumentation to a more generic mean. Mira reported that he was 'deeply disappointed' at the changes which he was expected to make, which certainly not only reduce the extraordinarily kaleidoscopic colours which he habitually used, but condemned him to hard labour, as he did not have the money to pay an assistant, who might have done much of the 'donkey work' which the revisions entailed. He felt that he was being obliged to 'coarsen' his painstaking work.[369]

Nevertheless, on 5 March, having exerted himself at his composing desk even more than usual, certainly more than was advisable, Prokofiev was feeling *'on top of the world'*. The 'flu which had weakened him in the past weeks had lifted somewhat, and according to Mira Mendelson, he found himself in a positively joyful and optimistic frame of mind.[370] The previous winter of serious illness and financial insecurity had depressed him deeply, and the ensuing 'flu had been the last straw. His doctor had ordered him to bed and applied leeches; it had taken work to lift him from the doldrums.

This was a moment of enormous political uncertainty in Russia, and a great potential danger for anyone, particularly those in public life, close to the seat of power.

Stalin had known that he was dying for some time, and was convinced that the entire government was at risk of being poisoned by a cabal of Jewish doctors. On 15 January, he had arrested nine doctors, six of them Jewish, and they were accused of plotting against the Soviet Leadership.[371]

Stalin had for years been confined to one room; Svetlana, his daughter wrote:

'In one corner there stood a record player. My father had a good collection of Russian, Ukrainian and Georgian folksongs, and did not recognize the existence of any other kind of music.'

This descibes the range of musical tastes of the man whose criticism of Shostakovich's *Lady Macbeth of the Mtsensk District* in 1936, whose infallible opinions on all aspects of the modern had brought the development of 20th-century Soviet art to an almost complete standstill, and marooned Soviet new music in a creative backwater where it would remain until the late 1960s. Of course, it was hardly Stalin's attack on artistic freedom of expression which had made him so widely feared, but, within the Soviet musical world, his death was awaited with eager yet fearful anticipation. When the news of his death eventually broke, it created an unprecedented atmosphere of grief and relief, mixed with suspicion and euphoria.[372]

In those first few days of March, as the rehearsals of *The Stone Flower* continued apace at the Bolshoi, not far from the Prokofievs' Moscow apartment, the composer's condition worsened. Despite Mira's best efforts to lighten his mood and alleviate the gloom that hung over the apartment, his depression, his sense of failure, deepened. She was extremely worried:

'When I would ask him, as I did worry how he felt, and if he had pain anywhere, I would sometimes hear a very uncharacteristic reply from him: "My soul hurts".'[373]

Normally at this time of year, with spring nearing, the Prokofievs would have been at their dacha outside the city, at Nikolina Gora. Prokofiev's illness had confined them to the city for the whole of the winter, which can hardly have improved his mood, but it was vital that he be near his doctors.[374]

Prokofiev seated in the garden at Nikolina Gora

On the afternoon of his death, he was driven to a public park near the apartment for a walk. Moscow was snowbound, but the approach of spring was in the air. Prokofiev might well have longed for the colour of the flowerbeds at Nikolina Gora, as he drove through the miserable streets, filled with the dirty snow of the end of the Russian winter.[375] Ironically, whatever the title of his ballet, he was to be denied flowers to the last. At Prokofiev's funeral there would be no flowers; there were none to be had, not for love or money, in the whole of Moscow; every single bloom had been commandeered for the funeral of the great leader.[376] It was left to the pianist Sviatoslav Richter, who at the moment of Prokofiev's death was boarding a plane in the Caucasus, to place a single pine branch on the composer's bare coffin. He wrote:

At the moment that I climbed into the aeroplane which would take me from Tblisi to Moscow, I learnt that Prokofiev was dead. We had to land in Sulchimi. Unprecedented, heavy snow was falling ceaselessly on the black palms and the Black Sea. It was terrible. I thought of Prokofiev, but . . . I did not grieve.'[377]

Earlier that morning, Mira and Sergey had talked about going to their dacha.[378] Mira arranged with a local woman to go out to Nikolina Gora to open the summerhouse.[379] One senses that Mira would have been grateful for anything that alleviated her husband's growing sense of his own mortality. Perhaps the countryside would revivify him. Her own mood in recent weeks had not been improved by his insistence that she help him 'put his affairs in order'. In this as in his compositions, it was almost as if he hoped that he might cheat death through organization, through archiving and forward planning. To her considerable distress, despite her pleading with him to save his energy, Sergey made her take down a list of projected and unfinished works by dictation. The only work on the list that was achieved was a proposed revision of the *Fifth Piano Sonata*. He lamented what he perceived as the paucity of his output:

'I could, should have written so much more . . .'[380]

Stalin's death precipitated, as much as rejoicing, an hysterical outbreak of nationwide mourning; even those who were relieved by the death of the tyrant alternated between consoling their friends and acquaintances who were weeping, and periodically admonishing them to desist.[381]

On the afternoon of the 5 March, Lavrovsky stopped by at the Prokofievs' apartment on his way to the Bolshoi. 'Prokofiev worked,' he said, 'with all of his old vigour . . . he was sitting over the score of the *"pas de deux"*[382] of Katerina and Danilo. He seemed quite well.'[383] The Prokofievs' apartment was situated in the theatre and concert hall quarter, and was only five minutes walk from the Bolshoi Theatre; the composer Dmitri Kabalevsky had an apartment in the same block. Its proximity to the theatre was convenient, but unfortunately made it easier for the theatre to pressurize the ailing composer. Lavrovsky was extremely keen to see how the problematic duet was coming along, putting Prokofiev under the strain of finishing his revision work at some speed, and consequently breaking the promises that he had made to his doctor, Elena Teppler, not to work too hard. When Lavrovsky left, he promised to call back, or telephone, ostensibly to let Prokofiev know how rehearsals had gone that day, but more likely to check on the progress of his revisions.[384] Dr Teppler paid a visit, and Prokofiev interrupted his work so that she could give him a check-up, before, presumably, dropping her back at her clinic when he went out for his 'constitutional' in the car. That afternoon, he had promised Dr Teppler to be sensible about work:

'Don't worry, I promise to be a good boy and will not upset the regimen, although sometimes it is difficult to tear oneself from work.'

Prokofiev had no intention of sticking to the doctor's 'regimen'. Later in the day, the concert master of the Bolshoi Orchestra, Stuchewsky, dropped by to pick up the finished version of *The Stone Flower* '*pas de deux*', he also packed up some manuscripts to be sent to the Central State Music Library.[385]

With all these visitors, it is somewhat difficult to believe that the conversation would not have turned, at some point in the day, to the uneasy atmosphere in Moscow; the ever increasing anxiety over the rumours that were flying around the city that Stalin was in his final days. It was a state of curious limbo.[386] Families were divided in their reaction to the growing crisis. Glasov writes,

'Those who sobbed and wept (at Stalin's death) tried to do their

Prokofiev and Mira Mendelson on the balcony of the dacha at Nikolina Gora, 1946

best to be heard by their neighbours, whilst angrily whispering to their dissident relations that they would certainly ruin the family with incautious and irresponsible statements. In my opinion, those who dared express their hatred of the dead Stalin, even in the womb of their own families were in the minority.'[387] From a musician's point of view, the truer irony was that Stalin's opinionated ignorance was of far greater danger to music than any of his troublesome composers had ever been to the Soviet Union. Shostakovich had been reduced to putting his works of overtly Jewish symmetries, particulary his extraordinary *Fourth Quartet*, 'in the desk' until 'Uncle Joe' was dead.

On 8 March, the *New York Times* announced Prokofiev's death from a cerebral haemorrhage: 'Prokofiev's health had not been good in recent years, and he had suffered previously from a heart ailment.'

No Soviet newspaper carried any announcement of Prokofiev's death for three days after the news was made public in the United States.

Upon returning from his short excursion at about 6pm, Prokofiev went into his study to have a sleep on his divan.[388] Two hours after Prokofiev had left her at her clinic, Dr Teppler was summoned urgently back to the Prokofiev apartment.[389]

At about 8pm, Mira had been sitting in her parlour, giving instructions to the woman who had agreed to go and open up the dacha for the Prokofievs.[390] Further to their conversation earlier in the day, Mira and Sergey had decided that, as spring was approaching, the best thing for Sergey's health and state of mind would be for them to go out to Nikolina Gora. Upon returning from his outing in the afternoon, he had had a bite to eat, and then he lay down in his studio next door, where Mira presumed that he was now sleeping peacefully after the exertions of the day. Suddenly the door opened and Prokofiev appeared, shivering and pale, apparently about to collapse. Mira jumped towards him and grabbed him, trying to stop him falling over:[391] 'Forgetting myself, I instinctively took hold of his shoulders so that he wouldn't fall, and helped him back into his room so he could lie down on the divan.'[392]

Doctor Teppler was called back; meanwhile, Mira asked Prokofiev, who was now breathing very heavily, if he would like her to read something to him? She read him Asakov's recollections of Gogol, which was, after Chekhov and Pushkin, his favourite book.[393]

Prokofiev died close to nine o'clock on the evening of 5 March 1953. Within the hour, Stalin himself died, like the composer, of a cerebral haemorrhage.[394] Soon after the composer had drawn his last breath, friends started to arrive, led by Dmitri Kabalevsky, thunderstruck by the news; he had been in a meeting of the Composers' Union when he had been told.[395]

According to Prokofiev's Soviet biographer Nestyev, he 'lay in state' in the Composers' Union, on the next day, 6 March.[396] This would seem to be a euphemism, as no one outside the immediate circle of friends and musicians in Prokofiev's circle would have heard about the death, and in the wake of Stalin's demise it was very difficult to get through the checkpoints and police barricades that were being set up across Moscow in preparation for the huge state funeral. In point of fact the musical establishment had neglected Prokofiev in the few years running up to his death, reducing him to a state of near penury. When the young cellist Mstislav Rostropovich had come to visit Prokofiev in his apartment a year or so before his final illness, he was so appalled to find that the Soviet Union's leading composer did not even have enough money for food, and by the conditions in which he was living, that he bearded Khrennikov in his office at the Composers' Union, and shamed him into making Prokofiev a grant of 5,000 roubles.[397] This was typical of the daring altruism of Rostropovich, always willing to put his own safety and career at risk the service of an oppressed artist or a just cause; he was cut from a very different cloth from some of his older Russian colleagues.

Prokofiev's funeral was attended by forty friends and colleagues. The secular service at the Composers' Union was presided over by Dmitri Kabalevsky. The pianist Feinberg played Bach, and David Oistrakh played two movements of the great violin sonata dedicated to him, the Sonata on F minor Op 80.[398] Appropriately enough, one of these was the haunted descriptive movement, which Prokofiev himself described as 'The Wind in the Graveyard', and which would be an enormous influence on Shostakovich when he came to write his own violin sonata for Oistrakh's sixtieth birthday, nearly twenty years later. Amongst others Shostakovich, Lavronsky and the Armenian composer Karan Khachaturian spoke at the ceremony.[399] After the service, the funeral procession wound its way through Moscow streets, which were alive with workers labouring to prepare Stalin's rather grander ceremony. It was a dreary day, as the cortège arrived at the cemetery of the Novo-Nevicky Monastery, where Prokofiev was laid to rest near the grave of his oldest friend Myaskovsky.[400]

Prokofiev and Mira Mendelson in the garden of the dacha at Nikolina Gora in 1946

Ironically, on the tenth anniversary of this double death, it was not the great dictator who was celebrated. All the major newspapers carried editorials celebrating the music and life of Prokofiev, now recast as the Soviet composer *par excellence*. Stalin, the cobbler's son, was only remembered in the Georgian village of his birth.[401]

Serge Prokofieff

Notes

The items in the Bibliography are referred to here in abbreviated form by author and date of publication.

1 Gerald Abraham, 'Prokofieff als 'Sowjet-Komponist,' in *Musik der Zeit* (1953), pp. 35-40, here p. 35; see also Edward Lockspeiser, 'The Unknown Prokofiev' in *The Listener* (22 October 1953) p. 705.

2 Hermann Danuser, 'Die Musik des 20. *Jahrhunderts (Neues Handbuch der Musikwissenschaft 7)*, Laaber, 1984, p. 206; see Sigrid Neef, 'Wechsel der Perspektive: Zum Schaffen von Sergey Prokofiev,' in *Musik und Gesellschaft 37* (1978), pp. 523–527, and recent articles in *Beiträge* (1990) and *Symposion* (1992).

3 Notes (1933), in *Dokumente* (1965), p. 198.

4 'Composer, Soviet-Style,' in *Time* (19 November 1945), pp. 57–62, here p. 57.

5 Serge Moreaux, 'Mit den Augen des Freundes gesehen,' in *Musik der Zeit* (1953), pp. 25–30, here p. 26.

6 'Autobiography,' in *Dokumente* (1965), p. 134; see further Boris Schwarz, 'Arnold Schönberg im russischen Kulturleben,' in *Bericht über den 1 Kongress der Internationalen Schönberg-Gesellschaft 1974*, Vienna 1978, pp. 187–195, and Hans Oesch, 'Schönberg und die russische Aventgarde um 1920,' in *Bericht über den 2 Kongress der Internationalen Schönberg-Gesellschaft 1984*, ed R Stephan and S Wiesmann, Vienna, 1986, pp. 108–121.

7 Marginal annotations by Schönberg in his copy of Pfitzner's polemic 'Futuristengefahr'; see Hans Heinz Stuckenschmidt, *Schönberg: Leben, Umwelt, Werk* (1974); New edition Munich and Mainz, 1989, p. 211.

8 'Autobiography,' in *Dokumente* (1965), p. 148.

9 Alfred Heinrich Brockhaus, 'Rezension von Nestjew' (1962), in *Musik und Gesellschaft 13* (1965), pp. 364-366, here p. 365.

10 Schnittke (1990), pp. 6 and 11.

11 See the critical discussion of the religious community by Hans-Diether Reimer, *Metaphysisches Heilen*, Stuttgart 1966.

12 Written in a notebook which was discovered in Paris in 1957. Photo reproduction in Samuel (1960), pp. 128f. [German] trans of Sviatoslav Prokofiev's text in *Beiträge* (1990), p. 58.

13 Ibid.

14 Schnittke (1990), p. 11.

15 'Autobiography,' in *Dokumente* (1965), pp. 136f.

16 According to Michel Astroff, 'Bei der Arbeit belauscht,' in *Musik der Zeit* (1953), pp. 315f, here p. 32.

17 8 June 1909, in Nikolay Myaskovskiy, *Stat'i, pis'ma, vospominaniya*. 2 vols, ed Sergey Šlifsteyn, Moscow 1959 and 1960, vol 2, p. 259.

18 Interview in *The Musical Observer* (1918), in *Dokumente* (1965), p. 192.

19 To the music critic Peter Suvtchinski (Ettal, 22 December 1922), [German] trans from Russian by M Weiss, in *Beiträge* (1990), p. 56.

20 'Autobiography,' in *Dokumente* (1965), p. 140.

21 Interview in *Boston Post* (1919), in *Beiträge* (1990), p. 103.

22 Danuser 1984 (see note 2), pp. 119-121; see also his 'Die "Mittlere Musik" der zwanziger Jahre,' in *La Musique et le Rite Sacré et Profane, Actes du XIIIe Congrès de la Société Internationale de Musicologie* (Strasbourg, 1982); ed M Honneger and P. Prévost, vol 2, Strasbourg 1986, pp. 703–721; and his 'Zum Stilbegriff bei Sergey Prokofiev,' in *Symposion* (1992), pp. 75–89.

23 'Wege der sowjetischen Musik' (1934) in *Dokumente* (1965), p. 199.

24 To the violinist and musicologist Stefan Lakatos (9 September 1931). In 'Deux Lettres' (1968), p. 164; see *Dokumente* (1965), p. 153.

25 Ibid.

26 Ibid.

27 Astroff 1953 (see note 17), p. 32.

28 See Danuser (1979) and Malcolm H Brown, 'Nationalism and Internationalism in Prokofiev,' in *International Musicological Society: Report*

of the Twentieth Congress, Berkeley 1977, ed D Heartz and B Wade (Kassel et al, 1981), pp. 47–49; Klaus-Wolfgang Niemöller, 'Identität und Weltbürgertum: Der Internationalist Sergey Prokofiev,' in Symposion (1992), pp. 3–25; and Wsewolod Saderatzkij, 'Prokofiev und das russische Lied: Die Umgestaltung der Tradition,' Ibid, pp. 135–44.

29 Interview in The Musical Observer (1918), in Dokumente (1965), p. 192.

30 'Autobiography,' in Dokumente (1965), p. 129.

31 'Les Six' – the name given by the Hispanic scholar and music critic Henri Collet to a group of composers in France loosely associated around Jean Cocteau (Arthur Honegger, Darius Milhaud, Georges Auric, Germaine Tailleferre, Francis Poulenc, Louis Durey), with further reference to the 'Five' of the Russian nationalist 'Mighty Fistful' (see note 68).

32 'Wege der sowjetischen Musik' (1934) in Dokumente (1965), p. 200.

33 As in Beiträge (1990), p. 194.

34 Nikolas Nabokov, 'Erinnerungen an Prokofiev,' in Merkur 29 (1975), pp. 844–856, here p. 846.

35 Johannes Rau, in Grussworte, a supplement to Beiträge (1992).

36 The title of the 1981 German trans based on the American edition.

37 Prokofiev on Prokofiev (1981). Forward to the annotations, pp. 11f.

38 Prokofiev on Prokofiev (1981), p. 11.

39 Ibid, pp. 11f.

40 The chapters 'Youth' and 'After graduation from the Conservatory;' printed together with 'The Years abroad and after returning home,' the autobiographical account of the years up to 1936 referred to as the 'so-called little autobiography' in Dokumente (1965), pp. 18–181.

41 Prokofiev on Prokofiev (1981), p. 17.

42 Ibid.

43 Ibid, p. 18.

44 Ibid, pp. 15 and 26f.

45 Ibid, p. 28.

46 Ibid, pp. 28 and 30.

47 Ibid, p. 32; despite the composer's ironic warning, even his childhood pieces have often enough been subjected to personal interpretation.

48 Ibid, pp. 32f.

49 Ibid, p. 36.

50 Ibid, p. 41.

51 Ibid.

52 Ibid, pp. 44f.

53 Reinhold Glière, 'Erinnerungen an Prokofiev,' in Dokumente (1965), p. 331.

54 Ibid, pp. 331f and 334f.

55 A breakdown of melodies used later is provided in the annotations to the Index of early works in Dokumente (1965), pp. 569–571.

56 Prokofiev on Prokofiev (1981), p. 110.

57 Ibid, p. 158.

58 Quoted from Boris Schwarz in Music and Musical Life in the Soviet Union, 1917 to the Present, ed J Zahnder-Reitinger. 3 vols Wilhelmshaven 1982, p. 16.

59 To his father, 5 February 1905, in Prokofiev on Prokofiev (1981), p. 166.

60 Prokofiev on Prokofiev (1981), p. 166.

61 Testimony of the music scholar Alexander Ossovski, quoted from Sawkina (1984), p. 48.

62 Schwarz (1982 see note 59), p. 17.

63 In 1908, first published sections at a time in several newspapers simultaneously; reprints appeared all over the world, some 200 newspapers running the article in Germany alone.

64 Prokofiev on Prokofiev (1981), p. 147.

65 Hans Ferdinand Redlich, 'Mussorgsky Redivivus,' in Anbruch 11, Vienna 1929, pp. 70–78, here p. 71.

66 'After all, I have not painted over the original frescoes for ever in reworking the piece. If one day people become convinced that the original is better and more worth while, they will set this reworking aside and 'Boris' will again be performed using the old score.' Quoted from Le Fahlbusch's forward to Rimski-Korsakow, Chronik meines musikalischen Lebens (Leipzig, 1968), p. 15.

67 A group of nationally oriented Russian musicians in the second half of the 19th century, so designated by the critic Vladimir Stasov, and consisting of Mili Balakirev, Alexander Borodin, César Cui, Modest Mussorgski and Nikolay Rimski-Korsakov.

68 The five composers' wishes were supported personally by Glinka's sister Ludmilla Shestakov.

69 'Thoughts and Reflections,' cited in Nestyev (1962) p. 23.

70 *Prokofiev on Prokofiev* (1981), p. 274.
71 Ibid, pp. 144f.
72 Ibid, p. 270.
73 Ibid, pp. 144f.
74 Ibid, p. 279.
75 Ibid, p. 299
76 Ibid, p. 274.
77 See *Dokumente* (1965), p. 131.
78 *Prokofiev on Prokofiev* (1981), p. 149.
79 Quoted in Sawkina (1984), p. 37.
80 *Prokofiev i Miaskovsky* (1977); in some political and musicological texts the correspondence has been published in a shortened form.
81 17 June 1908. Ibid, p. 52.
82 Ibid; the composer later reworked the Andante and incorporated it into the *Fourth Piano Sonata.*
83 'Autobiography,' in *Dokumente* (1965), p. 130.
84 Nestyev (1962), p. 44.
85 Ibid, p. 45.
86 Ibid.
87 See Karl Schlögel, *Jenseits des Grossen October: Das Laboratorium der Moderne, Petersburg 1909–1921.* Berlin, 1988.
88 Peter Bürger, *Theorie der Avantgarde* (Frankfurt am Main, 1974), p. 44.
89 'Manifeste du futurisme,' in *Le Figaro* (20 February, 1909).
90 Zofia Lissa, 'Geschichtliche Vorformen der Zwölftontechnik,' in *Acta Musicologica 7* (1935), pp. 15–21, here p. 18.
91 Quoted from Jan Maegaard, *Studien zur Entwicklung des* dodekaphonen *Satzes bei Arnold Schönberg*, 3 vols (Copenhagen, 1972), vol 2, p. 123.
92 'Autobiography,' in *Dokumente* (1965), p. 128.
93 Nikolaj Mjaskovskij, 'Sergey Prokofiev Op 4 (1913),' in *Dokumente* (1965), p. 129.
94 *Prokofiev on Prokofiev* (1981), p. 370.
95 See ibid, pp. 350–354.
96 Slovo (20 December 1908). Quoted from 'Autobiography,' in *Dokumente* (1965), p. 129.
97 23 October 1916, in *Prokofiev i Miaskovsky* (1977), p. 145.
98 'Autobiography,' in *Dokumente* (1965), p. 134; by publishing with the Gutheil Press, which also belonged to Kussevizki's publishing company, Prokofiev was able to avoid this committee.
99 To Glière, 30 December 1910. Quoted from Nestyev (1962), p. 64.
100 Golos Moskvy (21 July 1911). Quoted from Nestyev (1962), p. 65.
101 Miaskovsky to Derzhanovsky, the editor of the journal *Muzyka*, 28 December 1911. Quoted from Nestyev (1962), p. 66.
102 'Autobiography,' in *Dokumente* (1965), p. 133.
103 Miaskovsky to Derzhanovsky, 26 December 1911. Quoted from Nestyev (1962), p. 66.
104 'Autobiography,' in *Dokumente* (1965), p. 138.
105 Ibid, p. 135.
106 See Richard Buckle, *Diaghilev*, [German trans by J Abel] (Hereford, 1984), pp. 281–284.
107 Harlow Robinson, *Sergey Prokofiev*, (North Eastern University Press: Boston, 1987)
108 'Autobiography,' in *Dokumente* (1965), p. 138.
109 See Gunhild Oberzaucher-Schüller, '"Schreiben Sie die Musik so, dass sie russisch ist" (Sergey Diaghilev): Der Ballett komponist Sergey Prokofiev in der ästhetischen Pflicht seiner Auftraggeber,' in *Symposion* (1992), pp. 207–249.
110 Quoted from Seroff (1968), p. 98.
111 *Diaghilev i russkoe iskusstvo* (1982), vol 2, pp. 299f; quoted from the [German] trans by J Maly, in Oberzaucher-Schüller (see note 109), p. 240 note 6.
112 'Autobiography,' in *Dokumente* (1965), p. 138.
113 Ibid, p. 139.
114 Ibid.
115 Ibid.
116 Leonide Massine, *My Life in Ballet*, ed P. Hartnoll and R Rubens (London, 1963), p. 171.
117 See '[…] if the most cultivated person he associates with is Tcherepnin,' in *Igor Strawinsky. Gespräche mit Robert Craft* (Mainz, 1961), p. 41.
118 Stravinsky, *Selected Correspondence*, ed Robert Craft, vol 2 (London / Boston 1984), p. 19; see *Gespräche mit Robert Craft*, '[…] and had him staying with us for two or three months. […] I want to bring him to see you. He must be completely changed, otherwise we will lose him forever.'
119 Ibid, p. 141.
120 Birževye vedomosti und Večernie

vremja (1916) in *Dokumente* (1965), pp. 190–192.

121 'Autobiography,' in *Dokumente* (1965), p. 191.

122 Ibid, pp. 141f.

123 Harlow Robinson, *Sergey Prokofiev*, (Boston, 1987), p. 123

124 'Autobiography' in Dokumente (1965), p. 158.

125 Harlow Robinson, quoting Prokofiev in his autobiography, pp. 158–159.

126 'Autobiography' in Dokumente (1965), pp. 145f.

127 Prokofiev himself did not want the term 'cantata' to be used. To him it seemed anachronistic. But in press the work was then published under that title, regardless of the composer's protests.

128 'Autobiography,' in *Dokumente* (1965), p. 146.

129 Ibid, p. 145.

130 Ibid, p. 148.

131 Ibid, p. 147.

132 Ossip Mandelstam.

133 'Autobiography,' in *Dokumente* (1965), p. 149.

134 Ibid, p. 151.

135 *The New York Times* (19 September 1918); there were also reports on Prokofiev's arrival in *Evening News* (19 September 1918), *Musical Courier* (26 September) and *Musical America* (28 September); see Malcolm M Brown, 'Prokofiev in the United States,' in *Symposion* (1992), pp. 41–56.

136 'Composer, Soviet-Style,' in *Time* (19 November 1945), pp. 57–62, here p. 57.

137 As Brown (see note 133) points out, in for example the 1990 / 91 season, works by Prokofiev featured on the pro-grammes in the concert series of nearly every major American orchestra.

138 Anisfeld took over the staging of the Chicago first production of *Love for Three Oranges*.

139 *Brooklyn Daily Eagle* (30 October 1918).

140 *The New York Times* (21 November 1918).

141 *Chicago Daily News* (7 December 1918).

142 *Boston Transcript* (21 November 1918).

143 *Opera News* (1 March 1919).

144 'On the production of *Tristan and Isolde* at the Maryinski Theatre (1909),' in Wsewolod Meyerhold, *Schriften, Aufsätze, Briefe, Reden, Gespräche*, 2 vols, ed A W Fewralski (Berlin, 1979), vol 1,

pp. 163–155, here p. 137.

145 'Autobiography,' in *Dokumente* (1965), p. 152.

146 Ibid.

147 See Eugen Szenkar, '*Die Liebe zu den drei Orangen*: Erste deutsche Aufführung Köln 1935,' in *Musik der Zeit* (4, 1953), pp. 54–56; after his expulsion by the Nazis, Szenkar was professionally active in Moscow between 1934 and 1937, as the leader of the Philharmonia and as a teacher at the Conservatory.

148 'Autobiography,' in *Dokumente* (1965), p. 161.

149 Ibid, p. 166.

150 In 1964 the opera was staged at the Maly Theatre in Leningrad, and in 1981, after an almost 50 year abstention, again in Moscow at the Stanislavski-Nomirovich-Dantchenko Music Theatre. See further Stephen Stompor, '*Die Liebe zu den drei Orangen*: Dokumente zur Aufführungsgeschichte,' in *Jahrbuch der Komischen Oper*, Berlin 9 (1969), pp. 7–15; and Harlow Robinson, 'Can Soviet Leaders Learn to Love Prokofiev's "Oranges"?' in *The New York Times* (12 April 1981).

151 See Nestyev (1962), p. 178.

152 'Autobiography,' in *Dokumente* (1965), p. 153.

153 Quoted from Nestyev (1962), p. 188.

154 'Autobiography,' in *Dokumente* (1965), pp. 157f.

155 Lina Prokofiev, 'Iz vospominanij' (From my recollections). Quoted from Robinson (1988), p. 172.

156 To Nina Košek, 11 July 1922 (Music Division Archives, Library of Congress). Quoted from Robinson (1988), p. 175.

157 Quoted from Neef (1988), p. 357.

158 The plot is set in the 16th century. In the literature reference is constantly made to the spirit of the Middle Ages. It cannot be stressed often enough that the Europe of the witch trials belongs to early modern times, linked to the supposedly scientific establishment of magic and belief in enchantment; see W D Mueller-Jahnke, *Magie als Wissenschaft*, Marburg, 1973.

159 Quoted from *Beiträge* (1990), p. 162.

160 Quoted from the libretto in German trans of *Der Feurige Engel*, opera in five

acts (7 scenes) after V Bryussov, text and music by Sergey Prokofiev (Bonn 1960), p. 26.

161 Fifth act, last scene, quoted from libretto, p. 43.

162 1 May 1928, in *Prokofiev i Miaskovsky* (1977), p. 276.

163 See Richard Taruskin, article on Prokofiev, Sergey in *The New Grove Dictionary of Opera*, ed S Sadie, vol 3 (London, 1992) pp. 1135–1141, here p. 1137.

164 25 January 1928. Ibid, p. 268.

165 'Autobiography,' in *Dokumente* (1965), p. 168.

166 Harlow Robinson, *Sergey Prokofiev*, (Boston, 1987), p. 178

167 Ibid, p. 159.

168 Ibid.

169 Ibid, p. 160.

170 Olin Downes, in *The New York Times* (15 June 1924).

171 'Autobiography,' in *Dokumente* (1965), p. 159.

172 Ibid, p. 160.

173 'Autobiography,' in *Dokumente* (1965), p. 160.

174 4 August 1925, in *Prokofiev i Miaskovsky* (1977), p. 216.

175 Ibid.

176 'Autobiography,' in *Dokumente* (1965), p. 161.

177 Ibid, p. 160.

178 Ibid.

179 Ibid, pp. 162f.

180 In the context of Prokofiev's biography, the title of the ballet based on the parable in Luke 15: 11–24 has become a metaphor of the composer's return to the Soviet Union.

181 'Autobiography,' in *Dokumente* (1965), p. 172.

182 The work process is described in Prokofiev's letters to the pianist between 8 June 1931 and 7 April 1933 and on 7 January 1935; Flindell (1971), pp. 427–430.

183 'Autobiography,' in *Dokumente* (1965), p. 174.

184 To Wittgenstein, 11 September 1931; Flindell (1971), p. 428.

185 'Autobiography,' in *Dokumente* (1965), p. 174.

186 Fritz Stege, 'Berliner Musik,' in *Zeitschrift für Musik 99* (1932), p. 1076.

187 'Autobiography,' in *Dokumente* (1965), p. 175.

188 See chapter headings in Nestyev (1962), p. 165: 'Years of Wandering Astray,' or in Brockhaus (1964), p. 52: 'The Prodigal Son.'

189 'Autobiography,' in *Dokumente* (1965), p. 148.

190 *Musical Leader* (19 December 1918).

191 'Autobiography,' in *Dokumente* (1965), p148.

192 *Diaghilev* (1982), vol 2, p. 129.

193 Anatolij Lunačarskij, *Musik und Revolution: Schriften zur Musik*, trans. from Russian and ed G Bimberg (Leipzig, 1985), and Anatolij Lunatscharski, *Die Revolution und die Kunst: Essays, Reden, Notizen*, selected from the Russian by F Leschnitzer (Desden, 1974); see Zofia Lissa, 'Lunatscharskis Ansichten über Musik,' in *Aufsätze zur Musikästhetik: Eine Auswahl* (Berlin, 1969), pp. 195–226.

194 Detlev Gojowy, *Arthur Lourié und der russische Futurismus*, Laaber, 1993.

195 Anton Haefeli, *Die Internationale Gesellschaft für Neue Musik* (IGNM): *Ihre Geschichte von 1922 bis zur Gegenwart*, Zürich, 1982.

196 See his well-grounded essay, *Mozart: A Study* (1930; Leipzig, 1975); new ed with a forward by A Csampai, Reinbek 1987.

197 'Aufführungen zeitgenössischer Musik sowjetischer und ausländischer Komponisten und Gastspiele ausländischer Interpreten' in Detlef Gojowy, *Neue Sowjetische Musik der 20er Jahre* (Laaber, 1980), pp. 420–441.

198 Nabokov (1975 as in note 35), p. 849.

199 8 March 1926 in *Prokofiev i Miaskovsky* (1977), p. 235.

200 *K novym beregam* (2 / 1923), pp. 15–17.

201 *New Majority* (25 October 1919).

202 *Chicago Herald* and *Examiner* (7 December 1918).

203 *Pacific Coast Musician*, Los Angeles (15 January 1921).

204 Interview in Riga (17 January 1927), in *Sovetskaya Muzyka* (4 / 1970), p. 115.

205 'Autobiography,' in *Dokumente* (1965), p. 165. Here 18 January is given as the date of the border crossing, but the diary gives 19 January.

206 19 January, *Soviet Diary* (1991), p. 9.

207 24 January. Ibid, p. 30.

208 Glasunov emigrated to Paris in 1932.

209 According to the account in the 'Autobiography' (in *Dokumente* [1965], p. 166), the work in question was Popov's well-known septet from the year 1927 (Galina Grigoryeva, article on Popov, in *The New Grove Dictionary of Music and Musicians*, ed S Sadie (London, 1980), vol 15, p. 85 describes the work as a sextet).

210 19 February. *Soviet Diary* (1991), pp. 105–107.

211 Boris Assafjew (1927), in *Dokumente* (1965), p. 304.

212 'Zizn'iskusstva,' Leningrad (1 March 1927). Quoted from Robinson (1988), p. 208.

213 4 February. *Soviet Diary* (1991) p. 50.

214 Nestyev (1946), p. 103.

215 Schwarz (1982 as in note 59), p. 193, note 11.

216 Robinson (1988), p. 204.

217 'Autobiography,' in *Dokumente* (1965), p. 161.

218 Ibid.

219 Ibid, p. 162.

220 'André George,' in *Nouvelles Littéraires* (21 June 1927). Quoted from Robinson (1988), p. 211.

221 'Autobiography,' in *Dokumente* (1965), p. 167.

222 Ibid, p. 170.

223 Meyerhold (1979, as in note 142), vol 2, p. 486.

224 Jurij V Keldyš, '"Stal'noi Skok" S Prokofieva,' in *Musykal' noe obrazovanie* (3 / 1928), p. 44.

225 Krzystof Meyer, *Dmitri Schostakowitsch* (Leipzig, 1980), p. 71.

226 16 May 1930. *Prokofiev i Miaskovsky* (1977), p. 330.

227 See Alexander Farbstein: *Realismustheorie und Probleme der Musikästhetik*, [German] trans from Russian by E Kuhn, ed E Lippold, Berlin, 1977.

228 Lev Lebedinskij, *8 let bor'by za proletarskuju muzyku / 1923–1931* (8 years of struggle for proletarian music / 1923–1931) (Moscow, 1931), p. 42.

229 Serge Moreaux, 'Mit den Augen des Freundes gesehen,' in *Musik der Zeit* (1953), pp. 25–30, here pp. 29f.

230 Gerald Abraham, in *Horizon 6 / 33* (September 1942), p. 243. Quoted from Schwarz (1982 as in note 59), pp. 215f.

231 *Sovetskoe Iskusstvo* (16 October 1932);

see Gojowy (1980 as in note 195), p. 58.

232 Ibid, p. 57.

233 Schwarz (1982 as in note 59), p. 204.

234 Copy of the Moscow and Leningrad discussions in *Sovetskaya Muzyka* (March and May, 1936).

235 Schwarz (1982 as in note 59), pp. 207ff; In 1963 Shostakovich's opera was reinstated under the new title 'Katarina Izmaylova,' and the *Pravda* critique rejected as superseded.

236 Igor Strawinsky, *Gespräche mit Robert Craft* (Mainz, 1961), p. 40.

237 Svyatoslav Prokofiev, 'Über meine Eltern,' interview with Natalie Sawkina, [German] trans from Russian by E Martinjuk, in *Beiträge* (1990), pp. 87–120, here p. 95.

238 Gojowy (1980 as in note 195), p. 38.

239 As in note 236.

240 Nabokov (1975 as in note 35).

241 Schönberg had at first himself toyed with the idea of moving to the Soviet Union.

242 *My Creative Answer* (1938); see Schwarz (1982) p. 283, note 54: 'The cogent words 'to justified criticism' do not however come directly from Shostakovich, but are taken from a Soviet review of his *Fifth Symphony*, which Shostakovich quotes approvingly.'

243 'Das Aufblühen der Kunst' (1937), in *Dokumente* (1965), p. 208.

244 'Mein Vater, seine Musik und ich,' [German] trans from Russian by A Puttfarken, in *Beiträge* (1991), pp. 79–86, here p. 83.

245 Contribution to *Isvestiya* (16 November 1934), in *Dokumente* (1965), pp. 199f.

246 Ibid, p. 199.

247 'Die sowjetische Musik und des Arbeiterpublikum' (1936) in *Dokumente* (1965), p. 200.

248 'Die Massen verlanger nach grosser Musik' (1937), ibid, pp. 206f.

249 'Eine ernsthafte Prüfung' (1937), ibid, p. 207.

250 Nestyev (1962), p. 261.

251 'Das Aufblühen der Kunst' (1937), in *Dokumente* (1965), p. 208.

252 Nestyev (1962), p. 251.

253 'Autobiography,' in *Dokumente* (1965), p. 178.

254 Boris Pasternak, who was condemned to silence as a writer between 1933 and

1943, devoted himself to translating Shakespeare during this period.

255 See Rudolf Pečman, 'Licht im Dunkel: Zur Brünner Uraufführung von Prokofievs Ballet *Romeo und Julia*,' in *Symposion* (1992), pp. 251–267.

256 See further Nestyev (1962), p. 289.

257 Nestyev (1971), p. 1334.

258 At the Maya Theatre in Leningrad in 1973, Oleg Winogradov took up Prokofiev's dramaturgical idea of having the lovers reawaken by framing the tragic action within a production by a ballet company, as a play within a play.

259 'Autobiography,' in *Dokumente* (1965), pp. 180f.

260 'Das Aufblühen der Kunst' (1937), in *Dokumente* (1965), p. 208.

261 See p. 97.

262 As for instance in the slow movement of the *Fifth Symphony*, in the opera *War and Peace*, the *Eighth Piano Sonata*, the *Seventh Symphony* and the ballet *Cinderella*. The music to 'Boris Godunov' op 70a was first performed in 1957, *Eugene Onegin* in 1980. In 1962 the conductor Gennadi Roshdestvenski put together an arrangement of 'Pushkiniana' out of music drawn from the three projects, op 70, op 70a and op 71.

263 Natalie Saz, 'Wie das Märchen "Peter und der Wolf" entstand' (1959), in *Dokumente* (1965), pp. 477-485; see also 'Das Moskaner Theater für Kinder,' in *Das Neue Russland* 6 / 3-4 (1929), pp. 42f, and Lili Körber, 'Das Theater für Kinder in Moskau,' ibid, 7 / 7-8 (1930), pp. 41f.

264 Quoted from Nestyev (1962), p. 263.

265 In *Abrisse des sowjetischen Musikschaffens*, p. 77; quoted from Nestyev (1962), p. 265.

266 Nestyev (1962), p. 262.

267 Robinson (1988), p. 322, and Robinson (1985).

268 Danuser (1984, as in note 2), pp. 234–246.

269 'Was für einen Stoff ich suche' (1932), in *Dokumente* (1965), p. 196.

270 'Semjon Kotko' (1940), in *Dokumente* (1965), p. 219.

271 Reprinted in Juri Jelagin, *Taming of the Arts (Zähmung der Künste)*, [German] trans from English by H D Müller, Stuttgart, 1954.

272 First publication of the authentic shorthand report in *Teatr* (2 / 1974). See Vsevolod Meyerhold, *Ecrits sur le théâtre*, vol 4 (1936–1940), ed B Picon-Vallin (Lausanne, 1992), pp. 283–294.

273 The wording of the sentence from the KGB's archives was published by the journal *Teatralnaya Yizn* (2 / 1990); see Meyerhold, *Ecrits*, pp. 302f.

274 In 1955 the circumstances of his execution were finally made available, the illegality of his arrest acknowledged and the producer publicly rehabilitated. In the field of Prokofiev biography, the intimate correspondence between the two artists which they carried on for decades was suppressed for much longer. Nestyev (1962) only mentions Meyerhold in passing. Brockhaus (1964) makes no mention of him. In the comprehensive compendium *Dokumente* (1965) his name occurs in one solitary footnote. Sawkina (1984) mentions him in one sentence. See however Alexandre Fevral'kiy, 'Prokofiev i Meiercho'ld,' in *Stat'i i Materialy* (1965), pp. 108ff and especially Robinson (1986).

275 Oleg Prokofiev (1991, as in note 243), p. 85.

276 Quoted from Alexander Werth, *Russland im Krieg 1941–1945*, [German] trans from English by D Kiehl (Munich / Zurich, 1965), p. 104.

277 Quoted from Brockhaus (1964), p. 141.

278 'Der Künstler und der Krieg' (1944) in *Dokumente* (1965), p. 226.

279 Ibid, p. 229.

280 'A few words occasioned by the book *War and Peace*,' [German] trans from Russian by M Bräuer, in Lev Tolstoy, *War and Peace*, vol 2 (*Gesammelte Werke in zwanzig Bänden* 5), Berlin 1987, p. 789.

281 'Der Künstler und der Krieg' (1944), in *Dokumente* (1965), p. 226.

282 Quoted from Robinson (1988), p. 458.

283 Mira Mendelson-Prokofieva, 'Poslednie dni' (Last Days), in *Stat'i i Materialy* (1965), p. 282.

284 From a discussion between Lenin and Lunacharski reported in a letter from Lunacharski to Boltianski in *Lenin i kino*, ed G M Boltianski (Moscow / Leningrad, 1925), pp. 16-19.

285 See M Pleynet, 'The 'Left Front' of Art: Eisenstein and the Old 'Young

Hegelians," in *Screen* 13 (1972), pp. 103 ff.

286 'Autobiography,' in *Dokumente* (1965),
     p. 176.

287 Ibid.

288 Sergey Eisenstein, 'Patriotizm – moya
     tema,' in *Izbrannye proizvedeniya v šest
     tomach* 1 (1964), pp. 161–163, here 161.

289 'Die Musik zu "Alexander Newski"'
     (1943) in *Dokumente* (1965), p. 212.

290 Ibid.

291 Sergey Eisenstein: . . . *und fand sich
     berühmt*. Vienna / Düsseldorf, 1968),
     p. 324.

292 'Die Musik zu "Alexander Newski"'
     (1943) in *Dokumente* (1965), p. 212.

293 Zofia Lissa, 'Ästhetische Funktionen
     des musikalischen Zitats,' in *Die
     Musikforschung* 13 (1966), pp. 364–378,
     here p. 369.

294 Theodor W Adorno / Hanns Eisler:
     Komposition für den Film, ed and
     annotated by Eberhard Klemm
     (Leipzig, 1977), pp. 203–210; and Helga
     de la Motte-Haber / Hanns Emons,
     *Filmmusik: Eine systematische
     Bestandsaufnahme* (Munich / Vienna,
     1980), pp. 71–78.

295 In *The Film Sense*, ed Jan Leyda
     (New York, 1942), reissued 1970.

296 Marie Seton, *Sergey Eisenstein* (London,
     1952), p. 380.

297 N Klejman and M Nestyewa, 'Eisenstein
     und die Musik,' in *Kunst und Literatur* 28
     (1980), pp. 654–668, here p. 655.

298 3 October 1942, in *Prokofiev i Miaskovsky*
     (1977), p. 461.

299 'Sergey Eisenstein: Der Autor und sein
     Thema' (1944), in *Yo – ich selbst.
     Memoiren*. 2 vols, ed N Klejman and
     Walentina Korschunowa, vol 2
     (Frankfurt am Main, 1988), p. 962.

300 'Unsere Arbeit am Film' (1945), quoted
     from Eckhard Weise, *Sergey M Eisenstein
     in Selbstzeugnissen und Bilddokumenten*
     (Reinbek, 1975), p. 121.

301 'Die Zusammenarbeit mit Eisenstein'
     (1945), in *Dokumente* (1965), p. 233.

302 Zofia Lissa, *Ästhetik der Filmmusik*
     (Berlin, 1965), pp. 196 and 226f.

303 Quoted from Weise (1975 as in note
     299), p. 125.

304 See the positive assessment of the
     dictator and the unalleviated propagan-
     dist pathos of the appeal to hold out,
     in Andrey Tolstoy's drama in two
     parts, *Ivan the Fourth* (1944), which

was enthusiastically acclaimed by
official Soviet criticism.

305 24 April 1943, in *Prokofiev i Miaskovsky*
     (1977), p. 467.

306 Quoted from Schwarz (1982 as in note
     59), p. 304.

307 3 October 1942, in *Prokofiev i Miaskovsky*
     (1977), p. 461.

308 'Der Künstler und der Krieg' (1944),
     in *Dokumente* (1965), p. 230.

309 Swjatoslaw Richter, 'Über Prokofiev,'
     in *Dokumente* (1965), p. 440.

310 Boris Wolski, 'Prokofievs Filmmusik'
     (1954), in *Dokumente* (1965), p. 503.

311 Swjatoslaw Richter, 'Über Prokofiev,' in
     Dokumente (1965), p. 445.

312 'Meine Werke während des Krieges'
     (1945), in *Dokumente* (1965), p. 234.

313 'Musik und Leben' (1951), in *Dokumente*
     (1965), p. 236.

314 Ibid.

315 As in note 311.

316 'Die sowjetische Musik in den Tagen
     des Krieges,' keynote paper at the
     plenary meeting of the Organisational
     Committee of the Union of Soviet
     Composers (1944), in *Dmitri
     Schostakowitsch*: *Erfahrungen, Aufsätze,
     Erinnernungen, Reden, Diskussionsbeiträge,
     Interviews, Briefe*. [German] trans from
     the Russian by Chr Hellmundt, ed Krz
     Meyer (Leipzig, 1983) pp. 52–77, here
     p. 59.

317 A play on words alluding to the purges
     of the 'Yeshovshtchina' 1936–1938.

318 *Pravda* (29 November 1945).

319 *Sovetskoe Iskusstvo* (17 January 1947).

320 See Gleb Struve, *History of Soviet
     Literature* (Geschichte der
     Sowjetliteratur), [German] trans from
     English by H Neerfeld and G Schäfer
     (Munich, 1957), pp. 394 ff.

321 Stalin had of course always designated
     internationalism as the 'Unity and
     brotherhood of the proletarians and
     the nations of Russia;' see 'Marxism
     and the National Question (1913), in
     Joseph W Stalin, *Werke*, German ed,
     vol 2 (Berlin, 1950), p. 267.

322 'Eine Erzählung der Tapferkeit des
     Menschen' (1947), in *Dokumente* (1965),
     p. 235.

323 Programme note to the Moscow
     première on 25 December 1947. Quoted
     from Alexander Werth, *Musical Uproar
     in Moscow* (London, 1949), p. 25.

324 Werth (1949).

325 The individual papers from this conference are documented in ibid above.

326 *Pravda* (11 February 1948). In German in Karl Laux, *Die Musik in Russland und in der Sowjetunion* (Berlin, 1958), pp. 407–412.

327 Ibid, p. 408.

328 *Sovetskaya Muzyka* (1 and 2 / 1948).

329 *Sovetskaya Muzyka* (1 / 1948), pp. 9–26; see Andrej Shdanow, *Ausgewählte Reden zu Kunst, Wissenschaft und Politik* (Berlin, 1972), pp. 62ff.

330 'Tridcat' let sovetsoy muzyki i zadači sovetskich kompozitorov' (Thirty years of Soviet music and the tasks of Soviet composers) in *Sovetskaya Muzyka* (2 / 1948), pp. 23–46; see Werth (see note 322), pp. 89ff.

331 In *Hudebni rozhledy* (Prague, 1948), pp. 40f. Translated from Czech in *Les Lettres Francaises* (7 October 1948).

332 'Gesellschaftliche Grundfragen der modernen Musik' (paper delivered at the Prague conference on 23 May, in *Aufbau* 4 / 7 (1948), pp. 550–558. Reprinted in a version revised by Eisler as the Prague Manifesto, in Hans Eisler, *Musik und Politik: Schriften 1948–1962*, ed and annotated by G Mayer (Leipzig, 1982), pp. 13–31.

333 'Die gegängelte Musik,' in *Dissonanzen: Musik in der verwalteten Welt* (Göttingen, 1958), pp. 46–61.

334 'The Artist and his Conscience' (forward to Leibowitz 1950, see ensuing footnote.); in German in *Porträts und Perspektiven* (Hamburg, 1968), pp. 15–31; see Sartre, 'La musique nous donne une possibilité de capter le monde tel qu'il fut,' interview with Lucien Malson, in *Le Monde* (28 July 1977).

335 *L'artist et sa conscience: Esquisse d'une dialectique de la conscience artistique*, with a forward by Jean Paul Sartre (Paris, 1950).

336 See the contributions to the conference held by the Institute for New Music and Music Education in Darmstadt in 1969, in *Musik und Politik*, ed R Stephan (Mainz, 1971). A summary of discussion since 1948 is given by Miroslav K Černy, 'Ke kritikám "Pazkého manifestu," in *Hudebni Veda* 10 (1973), pp. 234–243 and 326–338 (Ms Eva Bayova's trans of this article from Czech is hereby gratefully acknowledged).

337 *Sovetskaya Muzyka* (1 / 1948), p. 56.

338 *Sovetskaya Muzyka* (12 / 1948), pp. 66f. Quoted from the [German] trans by H Lüdemann, in *Beiträge*, (1990), pp. 54f.

339 See Robinson (1988), p. 470.

340 From the obituary in *Der Spiegel* 43 / 3 (16 January 1989), p. 188.

341 Marina Sabinina, 'Eine Oper von S Prokofiev, die nicht geschrieben wurde.

Die Entwürfe zur Oper *Khan Busai*,' [German] trans from Russian, in *Kunst und Literatur* 10 (1962), pp. 1308–1321.

342 'Eine Erzählung von der Tapferkeit des Menschen' (1947) in *Dokumente* (1965), p. 235.

343 In the novel and also in the opera: Meressyev.

344 *Sovetskaya Muzyka* (1 / 1949), pp. 23–37 and (2 / 1949), pp. 7–36.

345 Sergey Schlifstein, 'Sergey Prokofiev und seine Oper *Der wahre Mensch*,' [German] trans from Russian, in *Kunst und Literatur* 9 (1961), pp. 676–689, here p. 688.

346 Mstislaw Rostropowitsch, 'Begegnungen mit Prokofiev,' in *Dokumente* (1965), p. 447; see also Mstislaw und Galina Rostropowitsch, *Die Musik und unser Leben,* compiled by C Samuel, [German] trans from French by A Lellemand. (Munich / Mainz 1985), pp. 77f.

347 Nestyev (1962), p. 376.

348 See Dusella (1990).

349 'Musik und Leben,' in *Dokumente* (1965), pp. 236f.

350 'Die Begegnung von Wolga und Don,' in *Dokumente* (1965), p. 239.

351 Brown (1977), p. 322. Notes 85 and 86 record 9 am as the time of Prokofiev's death based on his death certificate, and 9.30 am as the time of Stalin's death based on the report in *Pravda* on 6 March. The difficulties of arranging Prokofiev's memorial service and funeral are described by Galina Vischnovskaya, *Galina: Memoirs of a Primadonna* (Galina Wischnewskaja, *Galina: Memoiren einer Primadonna*), [German] trans from English by C Müller (Bergisch-Gladbach, 1986; new edition, Munich / Mainz, 1993), pp. 92f.

352 Mira Mendel'son Prokofieva,

'Posledniye dni' (The Last Days) in *Stat'i i Materialy* (1962 / 1965), p. 292.

353 *Sovetskaya Muzyka* (8 / 1953).

354 Shostakovich said in discussing the matter that the work expresses the 'optimistic vitality of youth' (ibid); Nestyev (1959), p. 396 mentions that the original plan was to compose a symphony for children; Brown (1967), p. 456, note 1 connects this plan, based on a remark made in an interview by Mira Mendelson, with Prokofiev's desire to be able to justify the simplicity required officially on aesthetic grounds.

355 Ulrich Dibelius, 'Prokofiev – ein Symphoniker?' in *Philharmonische Blätter*, Berlin (1979–80), booklet 4, pp. 2–5, here p. 2.

356 Olin Downes, 'Prokofiev's *Seventh*,' in *The New York Times* (26 April 1953).

357 Brown (1967), p. 463.

358 Edward Lockspeiser, 'Prokofiev's *Seventh Symphony*,' in *Tempo* 37 (1955), pp. 24–27, here p. 24.

359 'Autobiography,' in *Dokumente* (1965), p. 146.

360 As in note 357.

361 'Autobiography,' in *Dokumente* (1965), p. 145.

362 Dmitri Kabalewski, 'Sergey Prokofiev (1952), in *Dokumente* (1965), p. 400.

363 Yuri Glasov, in *Sovietica –The Russian Mind Since Stalin's Death* vol. 47 (reprint, Dordrecht, Boston, Lancaster: D Reidel, 1985), p. 6.

364 Victor Seroff, in *Sergey Prokofiev, a Soviet Tragedy* (reprint, London: Leslie Frewin, 1968), p. 339.

365 Lawrence and Elizabeth Hanson, in *Prokofiev – the prodigal son* (reprint, Lonon: Cassell, 1964), p. 223.

366 Michel R. Hoffmann, in *Serge Prokofiev* (reprint, Paris: Segher, 1963), 72.

367 Seroff, p. 359.

368 Seroff, p. 37.

369 Harlow Robinson, in *Sergey Prokofiev –*
a Biography (reprint, New York: Viking, 1987), p. 492.

370 Hoffmann, p. 72.

371 Alison Macleod, in *The death of Uncle Joe* (reprint, Woodbridge, Suffolk: Merlin Press, 1997), p. 37.

372 Glasov, p. 9.

373 Robinson, p. 292.

374 Daniel Jaffé, in *Sergey Prokofiev* (reprint, London: Phaidon, 1998), p. 211.

375 Michel Dorigné, in *Serge Prokofiev* (reprint, Paris: Fayard, 1994), p. 711.

376 Jaffé, p. 212.

377 Sviatoslov Richter, in *S. Prokofiev – Materials, Articles, interviews* Ed.Vlad Blok, Trans. Andrew Markow, (progress Publishers, 1978), p. 195.

378 Jaffé, p. 212.

379 Robinson, p. 493.

380 Robinson, p. 492.

381 Glasov, p. 2.

382 Hanson, p. 223.

383 Hoffman, pp. 72–3.

384 Seroff, p. 359.

385 Robinson, p. 493.

386 Glasov, p. 6.

387 Nestyev, in *Prokofiev* (reprint, Stanford, California: Stanford University Press, 1960), p. 437.

388 Seroff, p. 359.

389 Robinson, p. 493.

390 Dorigné, pp. 711–12.

391 Robinson, p. 493.

392 Jaffé, p. 210.

393 Nestyev, p. 437.

394 Hoffman, p. 72.

395 Glasov, p. 2.

396 Nestyev, p. 137.

397 Jaffé, p. 210.

398 Nestyev, p. 138.

399 Nestyev, p. 138.

400 Victor Seroff, in *Sergey Prokofiev, a Soviet Tragey* (reprint, London: Leslie Frewin, 1968), p. 360.

401 Nicolas Slominsky, in *Perfect Pitch* (reprint, Oxford: Oxford University Press, 1988), p. 231.

Chronology

Year	Age	Life
1891		11 (23) April 1891: Sergey Sergeyevitch Prokofiev is born in Sonzovka
1896	5	First attempt at composing: an *Indian Gallop*
1900	9	First opera *The Giant*
1902	11	Lessons with Pomeranzev; second opera *On Desert Islands*; beginning of composition lessons with Glière; first 'Pesenky' (Little Songs) (until 1907), and *Symphony* in G major
1903	12	Opera *The Feast in time of Plague* after Pushkin
1904	13	Prokofiev registers at the Conservatory in St Petersburg
1905	14	9 January: 'Bloody Sunday;' from Easter, interruption of studies for five months due to strike action
1906	15	Begins friendship with Myaskovski
1907	16	Completes the opera *Undine*
1908	17	*Symphony* in E minor and *First Piano Sonata*; debut at the 'Evenings for Contemporary Music' in St Petersburg
1909	18	Examinations followed by professional development courses (conducting, piano, opera school); *Four Études* and *Symphonietta*
1910	19	Moscow debut with first performance (FP) of *First Piano Sonata*; death of father; symphonic poems *Dreams* and *Autumnal, Choruses* for female voice after Balmont
1911	20	*First Piano Sonata* published as opus 1

History

1891	Building of Trans-Siberian railway begun. Shearers' strike in Australia
1896	Theodore Herzl founds Zionism. First Olympic Games of the modern era held in Athens.
1900	First Pan-African Conference. First Zeppelin flight
1902	Peace of Vereeniging ends Boer War. Anglo–Japanese alliance
1903	Bolshevik-Menshevik split in Communist Party of Russia. Pogroms against Jews in Russia. Suffragette movement begins in Britain. Wright Brothers' first flight
1904	France and Britain sign Entente Cordiale. Russo–Japanese War. Photoelectric cell invented
1905	Russian revolution against monarchy fails. Bloody Sunday massacre. Korea becomes protectorate of Japan.
1906	Algeciras Conference resolves dispute between France and Germany over. Morocco. Duma created in Russia.
1907	Anglo–Russian Entente. Electric washing-machine invented
1908	Bulgaria becomes independent. Austria-Hungary annexes Bosnia-Herzegovina
1909	Dreadnought programme. Young Turk revolution in Turkey. Model 'T' car produced by Henry Ford
1910	George V becomes king of Britain. Union of South Africa created. Japan annexes Korea.
1911	Parliament Act resolves constitutional crisis in Britain. National Insurance begins in Britain. Chinese revolution against imperial dynasties. Ernest Rutherford discovers the nuclear model of the atom

Culture

Oscar Wilde, *The Picture of Dorian Gray*. Paul Gaugin goes to Tahiti. Giacomo Puccini, *La Bohème*. Thomas Hardy, *Jude the Obscure*

Puccini, *Tosca*. Sigmund Freud, *Interpretation of Dreams*
Arthur Conan Doyle, *The Hound of the Baskervilles*.

Henry James, *The Ambassadors*

Jack London, *The Sea Wolf*. J M Barrie, *Peter Pan*. Anton Chekhov, *The Cherry Orchard*
Richard Strauss, *Salome*. Paul Cézanne, *Les Grandes Baigneuses*

Henri Matisse, *Bonheur de vivre*. Maxim Gorky, *The Mother* (until 1907)
Conrad, *The Secret Agent*. Rainer Maria Rilke, *Neue Gedichte*
Mahler, *Das Lied von der Erde* (until 1909). Cubism begins.
Strauss, *Elektra*. Sergey Diaghilev forms Ballets Russes. Rabindranath Tagore, *Gitanjali*. F
Constantin Brancusi, *La Muse endormie*. Igor Stravinsky, *The Firebird*. Forster, *Howard's End*.
Stravinsky, *Der Rosenkavalier*.

Year	Age	Life
1912	21	FP of *First Piano Concerto* in Moscow
1913	22	First trip abroad with mother: Paris, England, Switzerland; sensational FP of *Second Piano Concerto* in Pavlovsk
1914	23	Wins Conservatory's Arthur Rubinstein Prize; official graduation concert includes the *First Piano Concerto*; in London makes acquaintance with Diaghilev
1915	24	Rejection of the ballet *Ala and Lolli* by Diaghilev in Rome, who commissions another ballet, *The Buffoon*; in Rome gives first concert in the West with the *Second Piano Concerto*; starts on Dostoyevski opera *The Gambler*
1916	25	FP of *Scythian Suite* in Petrograd
1917	26	*Classical Symphony, First Violin Concerto, Fleeting Visions, Third* and *Fourth Piano Sonatas*
1918	27	In May Prokofiev leaves the Soviet Union and travels via Siberia and Japan to the United States
1919	28	Commission to compose the opera *Love for Three Oranges* for Chicago; meets Carolina Codina; long illness with scarlet fever and diphtheria.
1920	29	Travels in Canada and Europe; renews contact with Stravinsky and Diaghilev
1921	30	FP of *The Buffoon* in Paris for the start of the Diaghilev season; in October returns to the United States, FP of the *Third Piano Concerto* and *Love for Three Oranges* in Chicago
1922	31	In March Prokofiev leaves America and moves to Ettal; from there makes various concert tours through Europe; works on the opera *The Fiery Angel*
1923	32	Renews correspondence with contacts in the Soviet Union; concert tours; in September marries Carolina Codina (Lina Llubera) in Ettal; in December they move to Paris
1924	33	In February first son Sviatoslav is born; *Second Symphony*; death of mother in December
1925	34	In June FP of *Second Symphony* in Paris under Kussevizki; *The Steel Trot*; in December concert tour in America
1926	35	Until January, on American tour; in February première of the *The Steel Trot*; travels in Italy, meeting with Gorki in Naples and with Meyerhold in Paris; consultations over the forthcoming visit to Moscow
1927	36	January to March, first trip to the Soviet Union (Diary); gives concerts with Persimfans; in Leningrad meets young composers including Shostakovich and Popov. In April in Monte Carlo makes plans with Diaghilev regarding the ballet *The Steel Trot*; in May *Love for Three Oranges* produced in Moscow; in June FP of *The Steel Trot* in Paris and then London; *The Fiery Angel* is completed; *The Gambler* is revised in collaboration with Meyerhold

History	Culture
1912 Balkan Wars (until 1913). Titanic sinks.	Russell, *The Problems of Philosophy*
1913 Ulster Volunteers formed. Treaties of London and Bucharest.	Marcel Proust, *A la recherche du temps perdu* (until 1927)
1914 28 June: Archduke Franz Ferdinand assassinated in Sarajevo. First World War begins. Panama Canal opens.	James Joyce, *The Dubliners*. Ezra Pound, *Des Imagistes*.
1915 Dardanelles/Gallipoli campaign. Asquith forms coalition government in Britain. Zeppelin raids. Japan imposes 21 Demands on China.	Albert Einstein, *General theory of relativity*. Apollinaire, *Le poète assassiné*. Gorge Bernard Shaw, *Pygmalion*.
1916 Battle of Somme. Battle of Jutland.	
1917 Russian revolutions; Tsar Nicholas II abdicates and Communists take power.	First recording of New Orleans jazz. Franz Kafka, *Metamorphosis*.
1918 Second battle of Marne. 11 November: Armistice agreement ends first world war.	Oswald Spengler, *Decline of the West*
1919 Treaty of Versailles. Spartacist revolt in Germany. Comintern held in Moscow. Prohibition in US. Irish Civil War	Kafka, *In the Penal Colony*. The Bauhaus founded in Weimar.
1920 IRA formed. First meeting of League of Nations.	Edith Wharton, *The Age of Innocence*
1921 National Economic Policy in Soviet Union.	Aldous Huxley, *Crome yellow*. Chaplin, *The Kid*
1922 Soviet Union formed. Benito Mussolini's fascists march on Rome	T S Eliot, *Waste Land*. Joyce, *Ulysses*
1923 Ottoman empire ends; Palestine, Transjordan and Iraq to Britain; Syria to France	Le Corbusier, *Vers une architecture*
1924 Vladimir Lenin dies	Forster, *A Passage to India*.
1925 Pact of Locarno. Chiang Kai-shek launches campaign to unify China.	F Scott Fitzgerald, *The Great Gatsby*. Television invented
1926 Germany joins League of Nations. Antonio Gramsci imprisoned in Italy. France establishes Republic of Lebanon. Hirohito becomes emperor of Japan	Martin Heidegger, *Being and Time*. Virginia Woolf, *To the Lighthouse*.
1927 Joseph Stalin comes to power. Leon Trotsky expelled from Communist Party. Charles Lindbergh flies across Atlantic.	

Year	Age	Life
1928	37	In May FP of suite from the ballet *The Steel Trot* in Moscow; in June excerpts in concert from the opera *The Fiery Angel* in Paris under Kussevizki; in September the planned six-week trip to Russia is called off, as are two further trips planned for the winter; during the autumn Mayakovski and Meyerhold visit Paris; in December, second son Oleg is born
1929	38	In March the Diaghilev season in Monte Carlo opens with *The Prodigal Son*; in April FP of *The Gambler* in Brussels; in May FP of the *Third Symphony* and Paris première of *The Prodigal Son*; during the spring meets Mayakovski in Paris; in August Diaghilev dies in Venice. From October to November, visits Moscow; rehearsal for the ballet *The Steel Trot* at the Bolshoi Theatre cancelled following RAPM attack; in December, concert tour in America
1930	39	Until March Prokofiev continues concert tour through the United States, Canada and Cuba, then on to Europe; in May postpones his planned trip to the Soviet Union after Mayakovski's suicide; intensifies contacts in the West and for the first time moves into a permanent apartment in Paris. In November makes another trip to the United States; *First String Quartet*, ballet *On the Dnieper*; FP of *Fourth Symphony* for Boston Symphony Orchestra's 50th anniversary under Kussevizki
1931	40	In October, trip to Europe, *Fourth Piano Concerto* (for the left hand)
1932	41	In October, FP of *Fifth Piano Concerto* in Berlin under Furtwängler; in November Prokofiev pays a short visit to the Soviet Union for discussions about his return; accepts a lectureship at the Moscow Conservatory (until 1937); is commissioned to write the music for Fainzimmer's film *Lieutenant Kizhe*. In December 1932 travels across the United States and Europe
1933	42	In January returns from his trip; between April and June longer stay in the Soviet Union
1934	43	From April to June and November to December travels in the Soviet Union; has discussions about a ballet *Romeo and Juliet* with the Kirov Theatre in Leningrad
1935	44	Between March and October in the Soviet Union; in November and December travels with violinist Robert Soetens on concert tour through Spain, Portugal, Algeria and Tunisia; returns to Soviet Union in December
1936	45	From January to March goes on concert tour through Europe; in May family moves to the Soviet Union; *Peter and the Wolf*; from November, concert tour through Europe and the US

History	Culture
1928 Stalin introduces first five year plan proscribing Soviet collectivisation. Kellogg-Briand Pact for Peace. Alexander Fleming discovers penicillin.	Maurice Ravel, *Boléro*. Kurt Weill, *The Threepenny Opera*. D H Lawrence, *Lady Chatterley's Lover*. Walt Disney, *Steamboat Willie*.
1929 Trotsky exiled. Lateran Treaty. Yugoslavia kingdom under kings of Serbia. Wall Street crash. Young Plan for Germany	Robert Graves, *Good-bye to All That*. Ernest Hemingway, *A Farewell to Arms*.
1930 London Round-Table Conferences on India. Mahatma Gandhi leads Salt March in India. Frank Whittle patents turbo jet-engine. Pluto discovered	W H Auden, *Poems*. T S Eliot, 'Ash Wednesday'. Faulkner, *As I lay Dying*. Evelyn Waugh, *Vile Bodies*.
1931 Spanish republic formed.New Zealand becomes independent.	
1932 Kingdom of Saudi Arabia independent. Kingdom of Iraq independent. James Chadwick discovers neutron. First autobahn opened, between Cologne and Bonn	
1933 Nazi Party wins German elections. Adolf Hitler appointed chancellor. Hitler forms Third Reich. F D Roosevelt inaugurated US president; launches New Deal	André Malraux, *La condition humaine*. Gertrude Stein, *The Autobiography of Alice B Toklas*.
1934 Night of Long Knives in Germany. Long March in China. Enrico Fermi sets off controlled nuclear reaction	Agatha Christie, *Murder on the Orient Express*. Henry Miller, *Tropic of Cancer*
1935 Nuremberg Laws in Germany. Philippines becomes self-governing. Italy invades Ethiopia	George Gershwin, *Porgy and Bess*. Marx Brothers, *A Night at the Opera*
1936 Rhineland occupied by Germany. Edward VIII abdicates throne in Britain; George VI becomes king. Spanish Civil War.	A J Ayer, *Language, Truth and Logic*. BBC public television founded.

Year	Age	Life
1937	46	Until February, continues concert tour; *Cantata for the 20th Anniversary of the October Revolution*, marches *Songs of our Day*
1938	47	From January to May makes last trip abroad; beginning of collaboration with Eisenstein on *Alexander Nevski*
1939	48	Begins work on the opera *Semyon Kotko*, and a *Toast to Stalin*; in June Meyerhold is arrested; during the summer meets poet Mira Mendelson in Kislovodsk; Prokofiev becomes Acting Chairman of the Composers' Union in Moscow
1940	49	In January première of *Romeo and Juliet* at the Kirov Theatre in Leningrad; in June FP of *Semyon Kotko* in Moscow; *Sixth Piano Sonata*, *The Betrothal in a Monastery*, begins work on *Cinderella*
1941	50	From March begins living permanently with Mira Mendelson; in June, [German]invasion of the Soviet Union; beginning of work on *War and Peace*; in August, evacuation to Nalchik, *Second String Quartet*; from December, in Tiflis
1942	51	Until May, continues in Tiflis; between May and December in Alma-Ata, working on film music and collaborating with Eisenstein over *Ivan the Terrible*
1943	52	January and February in Moscow, from February to June in Alma-Ata, where first draft of *War and Peace* is completed, followed by further revision of the opera *Ballad of the Unknown Boy*; in March, awarded first Stalin prize (second class) for the *Seventh Piano Sonata*; from June to October in Perm; return to Moscow in October
1944	53	*Cinderella*, *Second Violin Concerto*, reworking of Russian folk songs for voice and piano; in May, the performance of Shostakovich's First Piano Concerto in Moscow, with Prokofiev conducting and Shostakovich as the soloist. Summer at the House of Creativity in Ivanovo, where the *Fifth Symphony* and *Eighth Piano Sonata* are completed; in October FP in concert of *War and Peace* in Moscow
1945	54	In January makes last appearance as conductor in FP of the *Fifth Symphony* in Moscow; at the end of January has a fall which results in prolonged illness; in May, Germany capitulates; screening of the first part of the film *Ivan the Terrible*, but work on the second part ends. During the summer, *Ode to the End of the War*; in the autumn returns to Moscow; in October the first complete concert performance of the revised *War and Peace* is given, the work is divided in two and revisions are resumed in preparation for a planned full production; in November the *Fifth Symphony* is first performed in America under Kussevizki, and *Cinderella* is performed at the Bolshoi Theatre in Leningrad

History	Culture
1937 Arab-Jewish conflict in Palestine. Japan invades China. Nanjing massacre.	John Steinbeck, *Of Mice and Men*. Picasso, *Guernica*
1938 Austrian Anschluss with Germany. Munich Crisis. IRA bombings in England.	Greene, *Brighton Rock*
1939 Stalin and Hitler sign non-aggression pact. 1 September: Germany invades Poland. Russo-Finnish war begins. Britain and France declare war on Germany.	Meyerhold dies. Steinbeck, *The Grapes of Wrath*. John Ford, *Stagecoach, Gone with the Wind*.
1940 Vichy government in France. Britain retreat from Dunkirk. Winston Churchill becomes PM in Britain. Battle of Britain	Hemingway, *For Whom the Bell Tolls*. Chaplin, *The Great Dictator*. Disney, *Fantasia*
1941 Germany occupies Balkans. Hitler abandons non-aggression pact; 22 June: Germany invades Soviet Union. Siege of Leningrad. US enters war.	Orson Welles, *Citizen Kane*. Messiaen to Paris Conservatoire
1942 Dieppe raid disaster. Battle of Stalingrad. Battle of Midway Island. Battle of El Alamein. Brazil enters war	Albert Camus, *L'Etranger*
1943 Allied bombing of Germany. Battle of Kursk. Allies invade Italy. Mussolini deposed and executed. Lebanon becomes independent	Sartre, *Being and Nothingness*. Eliot, *Four Quartets. Casablanca* with Ingrid Bergman and Humphrey Bogart.
1944 Normandy invasion. Paris is liberated. Arnhem disaster. Civil war in Greece	Jorge Luis Borges, *Fictions*. Eisenstein, *Ivan the Terrible*.
1945 Yalta Agreement. 8 May: Germany surrenders. United Nations formed. Clement Attlee becomes PM in Britain. Potsdam conference. Roosevelt dies; Harry Truman becomes US president. Atomic bombs dropped on Hiroshima and Nagasaki. Burma Road to China re-opened. 2 September: Japan surrenders. Wars of independence begin in Indo-China and Indonesia. Civil war begins in China	Benjamin Britten, *Peter Grimes*. George Orwell, *Animal Farm*. Karl Popper, *The Open Society and Its Enemies*.

| 1946 | 55 | In January, receives Stalin prize first class for the *Fifth Symphony*, the *Eighth Piano Sonata* and the music to the first part of the film *Ivan the Terrible*; during April / May celebrations are held in honour of the composer's 55th birthday. In June they move to Nikolina Gora; completes the *First Violin Sonata* begun eight years earlier; in June also, there is a closed stage première of *War and Peace* at the Maly Theatre; in July, receives the Lenin prize first class for *Cinderella*. In August Andrey Shdanov becomes head of the propaganda section of the Central Committee and Resolutions are passed regarding literature and theatre; in September Shdanov addresses the Writers' Congress; in November the FP of *Betrothal in a Monastery* takes place |

| 1947 | 56 | In June receives Stalin prize for the *First Violin Sonata*; in July the opera *War and Peace* is unexpectedly withdrawn, and after sharp criticism of the second part of *Ivan the Terrible* screening is forbidden. In the autumn, FP of *Festive Poem* and *Cantata for the 30th Anniversary of the Revolution* in Moscow; in November Prokofiev receives the honorary title of 'People's Artist of the Soviet Union;' begins work on the opera *The Story of a True Man*; in December, the Moscow first performance of the *Sixth Symphony* is affected by the Resolution, and a scholarly conference on the state of Soviet music is convened |

| 1948 | 57 | In January, marriage to Mira Mendelson; three-day conference of composers in the Central Committee of the Communist Party; in February, decree passed by the Central Committee regarding Muradeli's opera *The Great Friendship*, and the death of Eisenstein; in April a further conference of composers. In December a closed concert FP of the opera *The Story of a True Man* at the Kirov Theatre, but the opera is banned |

| 1949 | 58 | Collaborates with Rostropovich over the composition of the *Cello Sonata* |

| 1950 | 59 | In March, further serious illness; in August his friend Myaskovski dies; first draft of the ballet *The Stone Flower*, oratorio *Watch and Ward* |

| 1951 | 60 | In April, FP of *Ninth Piano Sonata* in Moscow to celebrate the composer's 60th birthday |

| 1952 | 61 | *Symphonia Concertante* and incomplete works, *Cello Concertino* and *Sixth Piano Concerto*; in February FP of the *Symphonic Cello Concerto* with Rostropovich conducted by Richter; in October FP of the *Seventh Symphony* |

| 1953 | 61 | New version of *Fifth Piano Sonata*, work on a *Cello Solo Sonata* and on the *Tenth Piano Sonata*, sketches and new plans; 5 March, death of Joseph Stalin and death of Sergey Prokofiev in Moscow |

History	Culture
1946 Cold War begins. Italian Republic formed. Juan Péron becomes president of Argentina. Jordan becomes independent.	Bertrand Russell, *Existentialism and Humanism*. Cocteau, *La belle et la bête*
1947 Puppet Communist states in eastern Europe. India becomes independent. Chuck Yeager breaks the sound barrier.	Tennessee Williams, *A Streetcar named Desire*. Anne Frank, *The Diary of Anne Frank*.
1948 Marshall plan (until 1951); Berlin airlift. Welfare state created in Britain. Malayan emergency begins (until 1960). Apartheid legislation in South Africa. Gandhi is assassinated	Greene, *The Heart of the Matter*. Norman Mailer, *The Naked and the Dead*. Alan Paton, *Cry, the Beloved Country*. Bertolt Brecht, *Caucasian Chalk Circle*.
1949 People's Republic of China created. Manchester MK I computer created	Orwell, *Nineteen Eighty-four*. Miller, *Death of a Salesman*.
1950 Schuman Plan. Korean War begins. China conquers Tibet. First successful kidney transplant.	Neruda, *Canto General*. Eugène Ionesco, *The Bald Prima Donna*. Billy Wilder, Sunset Boulevard.
1951 Anzus pact in Pacific	Stravinsky, *The Rake's Progress*. J D Salinger, *The Catcher in the Rye*.
1952 Gamal Abdel Nasser leads coup in Egypt. Britain refuses to join. US tests hydrogen bomb. Elisabeth II becomes queen of Britain. McCarthy era begins in US	Michael Tippett, *The Midsummer Marriage*. Hemingway, *The Old Man and the Sea*. Samuel Beckett, *Waiting for Godot*
1953 Stalin dies. Dwight Eisenhower inaugurated US president. Korean war ends. Francis Crick and James Watson discover double helix structure of DNA	William Burroughs, *Junkie*. Dylan Thomas, *Under Milk Wood*. Arthur Miller, *The Crucible*. Federico Fellini, *I Vitelloni*.

List of Works

First Piano Sonata in F minor op 1 (based on Sonata No 2 1907). Moscow, 21 February 1910 – *Four Studies* op 2 for piano. Moscow, 21 February 1910 – *Symphonietta* in A major op 5. 24 October 1915.

Two Poems op 7 (Balmont) for women's choir and orchestra. St Petersburg, 1910.

Dreams op 6 Symphonic poem for large orchestra. St Petersburg, 22 November 1910 – *Autumnal* op 8 Symphonic poem for small orchestra. Moscow, 19 July 1911.

Four Piano Pieces op 3. St Petersburg, 28 March 1911.

Magdalen op 13. Opera in one act. London, 25 March 1979 (orchestration by Edward Downes)

Four Piano Pieces op 4. St Petersburg, 18 December 1908.

First Piano Concerto in D flat major op 10. Moscow, 15 July 1912.

Toccata in C major op 11 for piano. Petrograd, 27 November 1916 – *Second Piano Sonata in D minor* op 14. Moscow, 23 January 1914 – *Ballade in C minor* op 15 for cello and piano. Moscow, 23 January 1914.

Ten Piano Pieces op 12. Moscow, 23 January 1914.

Second Piano Concerto in G minor op 16. Revised 1923. Pavlovsk, 23 August 1913. Paris, 8 May 1924 (revised version)

Sarcasms. Five Piano Pieces op 17. Petrograd, 27 November 1916.

The Ugly Duckling op 18. Petrograd, 17 January 1915.

Ala and Lolli. Ballet by Sergey Gorodezky and Prokofiev. Withdrawn and reworked into the (*Scythian Suite* op 20. Petrograd, 16 January 1916.

Humorous Scherzo for four bassoons op 12a (arranged after the piano piece from op 12). London, 2 September 1916 – *Five Poems* op 23 for solo voice and piano. Petrograd, 27 November 1916 – *The Buffoon (Le Chout)* op 21. Ballet. Théâtre de la Gaîté-Lyrique. Paris, 17 May 1921.

Five Poems op 27 (Ann Achmatova) for solo voice and piano. Moscow, 5 February 1917.

Fleeting Visions. Twenty Pieces op 22. Petrograd, 2 April 1918 – *The Gambler* op 24. Opera in four acts. Théâtre royale de la Monnaie Brussels, 29 April 1929.

First Violin Concerto in D major op 19. Paris, 18 October 1923 – *First Symphony* in D major op 25 (*Classical Symphony*). St Petersburg, 2 April 1918.

Third Piano Sonata in A minor op 28 ('From old Notebooks': *Sonata No 5* 1908 and *Symphony* 1908). Petrograd, 17 April 1918 – *Seven, they are* Seven op 30. *Chaldaic Invocation* (Balmont) for tenor, choir and orchestra. Revised 1933. Paris, 27 May 1924.

Tales of the old Grandmother. Four Piano Pieces op 31. New York, 7 January 1919 – *Four Piano Pieces* op 32. New York, 30 March 1919.

Overture on Hebrew Themes in C minor op 34 for piano, clarinet and string quartet. New York, 26 January 1920 – *Love for Three Oranges* op 33. Opera in three acts. Lyric Opera Chicago, 30 December 1921 – *Suite* from the opera *Love for Three Oranges* op 33a. Revised 1924. Paris, 29 November 1925.

Suite from the ballet *The Buffoon* op 21a, Brussels 15 January 1924 – *Five Songs without Words* op 35 (No 2 also in a version with orchestral accompaniment). New York, 27 March 1927.

Third Piano Concerto in C major op 26. Chicago, 16 December 1921.

Five Poems op 36 (Balmont) for solo voice and piano. Milan, May 1922.

March and *Scherzo* from the opera *Love for Three Oranges* op 33b for piano.

The Fiery Angel op 37. Opera in five acts. Teatro La Fenice Venice, 29 September 1955.

Fifth Piano Sonata in C major op 38. Revised 1952-53. Paris, 9 March 1924.

Trapeze. Ballet in one act by Boris Romanov. Berlin, end of 1925. Reworked as *Quintet* op 39. 6 March 1927.

Second Symphony in D minor op 40. Paris, 6 June 1925.

The Steel Trot (Le pas d'acier) op 41. Ballet in two scenes. Théâtre Sarah Bernhardt. Paris, 18 December 1930.

Suite from the ballet *The Steel Trot* op 41a, Moscow, 27 May 1928 – *American Overture in B major* op 42 for chamber orchestra. Arranged for full orchestra op 42a. 1928. Paris, 18 December 1930.

Five Kasak Popular Airs. Arranged for solo voice and piano.

Third Symphony in C minor op 44 (Material based on the opera *The Fiery Angel*). Paris, 17 May 1929 – *Things in Themselves (Choses en soi). Two Piano Pieces* op 45. New York, 6 January 1930.

Divertissement op 43. Paris, 22 December 1929.

The Prodigal Son (Le fils prodigue) op 46. Ballet in three scenes. Théâtre Sarah Bernhardt. Paris, 21 May 1929.

Sinfonietta in A major op 48. Third version of op 5. Moscow, 18 November 1930 – *Suite* from the ballet *The Prodigal Son* op 46a. Paris, 7 March 1931.

Fourth Symphony in C major op 47. Boston, 14 November 1930.

First String Quartet in B minor op 50. Washington, 25 April 1931 – *Andante* op 50a from the *String Quartet*, for string orchestra.

On the Dnieper (sur le Borysthène) op 51. Ballet in two scenes. Paris, 16 December 1932 – *Six Pieces* op 52. Moscow, 17 May 1932.

Four Portraits and *Finalé* from the opera *The Gambler* op 49. Paris, 12 March 1932 – *Fourth Piano Concerto in B major* op 53 (for the left hand). Berlin, 5 September 1956.

Two Sonatinas in E minor and G major op 54. London, 17 April 1932 (Second Sonatina) – *Fifth Piano Concerto in G major* op 55. Berlin, 31 October 1932.

LIST OF WORKS

Suite from the ballet *On the Dnieper* op 51a. Paris, 1934 – *Symphonic Song* op 57. 14 April 1934 – *Lieutenant Kijé*.

Three Piano Pieces op 59. Moscow, 1935 – *Reflections. Three Piano Pieces* op 62. Moscow, 13 November 1936.

Suite from *Lieutenant Kijé* op 60. Radio broadcast Moscow, 21 December 1934 – Two Songs op 60a for solo voice and piano – *Egyptian Nights*. Music for a play – *Suite* from the music for the play *Egyptian Nights* op 61a. Radio production Moscow, 21 December 1934 – *Andante* from the *Fourth Piano Sonata* op 29a. Arranged for full orchestra. 13 February 1958 – *Overture on Jewish Themes* op 34b, arranged for small orchestra. Moscow, 30 November 1934.

Second Violin Concerto in G minor op 63. Madrid, 1 December 1935 – *Music for Children. Twelve Easy Piano Pieces* op 65. Moscow, 11 April 1936 – Two Choruses op 66a. *Four Songs* op 66b for solo voice or unmixed choir and piano.

Romeo and Juliet op 64. Ballet in four acts. Theatre Brünn, 30 December 1938.

First Suite from the ballet *Romeo and Juliet* op 64a. Moscow, 24 November 1936 – *Second Suite* from the ballet *Romeo and Juliet* op 64b. Leningrad, 15 April 1937 – *Peter and the Wolf* op 67. Moscow, 2 May 1936 – *The Queen of Spades* op 70. *Boris Gudonov* op 70a. Meyerhold Theatre, Moscow. *Russian Overture* op 72 for four orchestras. Revised for three orchestras 1937. Moscow, 29 October 1936 – *Three Romances* op 73. Radio production, 20 April 1937.

Four Fairy Tales op 69 for wind orchestra.

Cantata for the 20th anniversary of the Great Socialist October Revolution op 74. Moscow, 5 April 1966.

Ten Piano Pieces op 75 from the ballet *Romeo and Juliet*. Moscow, 1937 – *Songs of our Time* op 76. *Suite* for solo voices, choir and orchestra. Moscow, 5 January 1938.

Cello Concerto in E minor op 58. Moscow, 26 November 1938.

Hamlet op 77. Music for Sergey Radlov's production of Shakespeare's tragedy. Drama Theatre Leningrad, 15 May 1938.

Gavotte op 77a for piano from the music for *Hamlet*. Moscow, 22 November 1939 – *Alexander Nevski*. Music to Sergey Eisenstein's film. *Divertissement* op 43a for piano.

Three Children's Songs op 68.

Alexander Nevski op 78. Cantata for mezzo soprano, choir and orchestra. 17 May 1939 – *Three Songs* op 78a – *Seven Songs* op 79 – *Semyon Kotko* op 81. Opera in five acts. Stanislavski Theatre Moscow, 23 June 1940 – *A Toast to Stalin* op 85. Cantata. Moscow, 21 December 1939.

Sixth Piano Sonata in A major op 82. Moscow, 26 November 1940.

The Betrothal in a Monastery op 86. Lyrical comic opera in four acts. National Opera Prague, 5 May 1946.

Summer Day op 65a. Children's suite for small orchestra – *Suite* from the opera *Semyon Kotko* op 81a. Moscow, 23 June 1942 – *Symphonic March in B major* op 88 – *Seven Songs for the Masses* and *March in A flat major* op 89 for solo voice and piano. Naltchik,

November 1941 – *March in A flat major* op 89a for wind orchestra – *The Year 1941* op 90. *Suite* for orchestra – *Lermontov. Second String Quartet in F major* op 92. Moscow, 5 September 1942.

Seventh Piano Sonata in A major op 83. Moscow, 18 January 1943.

Seven Songs for the Masses for solo voice (choir) and piano op 89 – *Three Piano Pieces* op 96.

Kotovski. Music to Alexander Fainzimmer's film – *Partisans in the Steppes of the Ukraine.* Music to Igor Savtchenko's film – *Tonya.* Music to Abram Romm's projected short film – *Khan Buzay.* Draft opera (unfinished) – *Three Pieces* op 95 from the ballet *Cinderella.*

Ten Piano Pieces op 97 from the ballet *Cinderella.*

War and Peace op 91. Opera in five acts. Moscow, 16 October 1944 (seven scenes in concert with piano accompaniment). Bolshoi Theatre Moscow, 15 December 1959 (13 scenes including epigraph).

Ballad of the Unknown Boy op 93. Cantata.

Flute Sonata in D major op 94. Moscow.

Eighth Piano Sonata in B major op 84. Moscow, 30 December 1944.

Cinderella op 87. Ballet in three acts. Bolshoi Theatre Moscow, 21 November 1945.

Second Violin Sonata in D major op 94a (Transcription of the *Flute Sonata*). Moscow, 17 June 1944 – *March in B major* op 99 for wind orchestra. Moscow, 14 May 1944.

Adagio op 97a from the ballet *Cinderella* for cello and piano. Radio performance Moscow, 19 April 1944 – *Fifth Symphony in B major* op 100. Moscow, 13 January 1945 – *Six Piano Pieces* op 102 from the ballet *Cinderella* – *Twelve Russian Folksongs* op 104. Two booklets. Moscow, 25 March 1945.

Ode to the End of the War op 105. Moscow, 12 November 1945 – *Two Duets* op 106. Arrangement of Russian folksongs for tenor, bass and piano op 106.

First Violin Sonata in F minor op 80. Moscow, 23 October 1946.

Ivan the Terrible op 116. Music to Sergey Eisenstein's film, 1946.

Third Suite from the ballet *Romeo and Juliet* op 101. Moscow, 8 March 1946 – *First Suite* from the ballet *Cinderella* op 107. Moscow, 12 November 1946 – *Second Suite* from the ballet *Cinderella* op 108 – *Third Suite* from the ballet *Cinderella* op 109. Radio performance Moscow, 3 September 1947 – *Waltz Suite* op 110. Moscow, 13 May 1947.

Sixth Symphony in E flat minor op 111. Leningrad, 11 October 1947.

Fourth Symphony in C major op 112. Revised version 1947 – *Ninth Piano Sonata in C major* op 103. Moscow, 21 April 1951 – *Thirty Years* op 113. Festive Poem for orchestra. Moscow, 3 October 1947 – *Bloom forth, Mighty Land* op 114. Moscow, 12 November 1947 – *Sonata for Solo Violin in D major* op 115, Moscow, 10 March 1960.

The Story of a True Man op 117. Opera in four acts. Kirov Theatre Leningrad, 3 December 1948. Bolshoi Theatre Moscow, 8 October 1960.

Cello Sonata in C major op 119. Moscow, 1 March 1950 – *Pushkin Waltzes* op 120 No 1 in F major and No 2 in C sharp minor for orchestra.

The Tale of the Stone Flower op 118. Ballet in four acts. Bolshoi Theatre Moscow, 12 February 1954.

Winter Log Fire op 122. *Suite*. Moscow 19 December 1950.

Soldiers' Marching Song op 121 – *Summer Night* op 123. *Suite* – *Watch and Ward* op 124. Oratorio. Moscow, 19 December 1950.

Symphonia Concertante for cello and orchestra in E minor op 125 (rewriting of op 58). Moscow, 18 February 1952.

Marriage Suite op 126 from the ballet *The Tale of the Stone Flower*. Moscow, 12 December 1951 – *Gypsy Fantasy* op 127 from the ballet *The Tale of the Stone Flower*. Moscow, 12 December 1951 – *Ural Rhapsody* op 128 from the ballet *The Tale of the Stone Flower* – *The Mistress of the Copper Mountain* op 129 from the ballet *The Tale of the Stone Flower* – *The Meeting of the Volga and Don* op 130. Festive Poem. Moscow, 22 February 1952.

Seventh Symphony in C sharp minor op 131. Moscow, 11 October 1952.

Concerto in G minor for cello and orchestra op 132 (unfinished, completed after the composer's death by Mstislav Rostropovitch and Dmitri Kabalevski).

Fifth Piano Sonata in C major op 135. Revised version. Alma-Ata, 2 February 1954.

Select Discography

Boris Godunov, Op 70 bis: Fountain Scene; Polonaise. Dreams, Op 6. Eugene Onegin, Op 71: Minuet, Polka, Mazurka. 2 Pushkin Waltzes, Op 120. Romeo and Juliet (ballet): Suite No. 2, Op 64. Chan. 8472. SNO, Järvi

Cinderella (ballet; complete), Symphony No.1 in D (Classical), Op 25. EMI Dig./ADD double forte CZS5 68604-2. LSO, Previn.

Concertino in G min. for Cello & Orchestra, Op 132 (completed and orch. Kabalevsky & Rostropovich); Sinfonia concertate in E min. for Cello & Orchestra, Op 125; (ii) Cello Sonata in C, Op 119
Revelation mono RV10102. Rostropovich, (i) USSR SO, Rozhdestvensky; (ii) Richter

Piano Concertos Nos. 1–5. Double Decca (ADD) 452 588-2 . Ashkenazy, LSO, Previn.

Violin Concerto No. 2 in G min., Op 63. RCA (ADD) 09026 61744-2. Heifetz, Boston SO, Munch – GLAZUNOV; SIBELIUS: Concertos.

Romeo and Juliet (ballet), Op 64 (complete). Ph. 464 726 – 2 (2). Kirov O, Gergiev.

Symphonies Nos. 1–7. Chan. 8931/4. RSNO, Järvi

String Quartet No. 2 in F, Op 92. Testament mono SBT 1052. Hollowood Qt

Violin Sonata No. 1 in F min., Op 80. Orfeo (ADD) C489981B. D. Oistrakh, S. Richter

Piano Sonatas Nos. 2, 7 & 8. DG 457 588-2. Pletnev.

Alexander Nevsky (cantata), Op 78 (in English).
RCA (ADD) 09026 63708-2. Elias, Chicago SO & Ch., Reiner

Ivan the Terrible (complete film score). Ph. 456 645-2. Sokolova, Putilin, Kirov Op. Chor., Rotterdam PO, Gergiev.

The Fiery Angel (complete). Ph. 446 078-2 (2) (Video 070 198-3; LD 070 198-1). Gorchakova, Leiferkus, Pluzhnikov, Ognovanko, soloists; Kirov Op. Ch. & O, Gergiev.

The Love for Three Oranges (complete in Russian). Ph. 462 913-2 (2). Akimov, Kit, Diadkova, Morozov, Pluzhnikov, Gerello, Shevchenko, & Soloists, Kirov Op. Ch. & O, Gergiev.

War and Peace (complete). Ph. 434 097-2 (3). Gergalov, Prokina, Gregoriam, Borodina, Gerelo, Bogachova, Okhotnikov, Morozov, Kirov Theatre Ch. & O, Gergiev.

Picture Sources

The author and publishers wish to express their thanks to the following sources of illustrative material and/or permission to reproduce it. They will make proper acknowledgements in future editions in the event that any omissions have occurred.

The David King Collection: pp. vi, 31, 86, 103, 124; Corbis-Bettman-UPI pp. 89; The Lebrecht Music Collection: pp. 2, 7, 14, 18, 23, 32, 33, 35, 41, 42, 45, 49, 50, 53, 54, 56, 59, 70, 73, 83, 84, 85, 88, 90, 91, (pp. 90 and 91 courtesy of the Prokofiev family collection) 100, 110–11, 114, 115, 123, 127, 134, 138; Novosti: pp. 4, 20, 25, 30, 128, 144, 146, 149

Index·